College Bound

College
Bound

What
CHRISTIAN PARENTS
Need to Know About
Helping Their Kids
CHOOSE A COLLEGE

THOMAS A. SHAW

MOODY PUBLISHERS
CHICAGO

Library of Congress Cataloging-in-Publication Data

Shaw, Thomas A., 1959-
    Collegebound : what Christian parents need to know about helping their kids choose a college / Thomas A. Shaw.
        p. cm.
    Includes bibliographical references.
    ISBN-13: 978-0-8024-1242-3
        1. College choice—United States. 2. Christian college students—United States—Life skills guides. I. Title.

LB2350.5.S43 2005
                                                          2005013030

ISBN: 0-8024-1242-4
ISBN-13: 978-0-8024-1242-3

1 3 5 7 9 10 8 6 4 2

Printed in the United States of America

Contents

Acknowledgments

This book would not have been possible without the support and encouragement of my family. My wife, Carolyn, realized its value to thousands of families and willingly sacrificed to go the extra mile while I wrote in the evenings and weekends. Given her background in publishing, she was an invaluable source of insight on the content, as well as editorial and marketing expertise along the way. To our collegebound teens—Bobby, Cathy, Emily, and Andrew, my deep love and appreciation for your patience, understanding, and encouragement throughout this exciting journey.

Special thanks are extended to Becky Dykstra and Phil Van Wynen, who were kind enough to lend a critical eye to a draft of the manuscript as it was nearing completion.

My appreciation also goes to the Moody Publishers team, including Greg Thornton and Mark Tobey, who caught the vision for this book and its relevance and importance to

Christian families. Also, I'm grateful to Ali Childers for her role in editing and strengthening it for readers.

Finally, I would like to acknowledge friends, colleagues, and professors who have helped mold my professional experience and education to the point of being able to assimilate the various perspectives of *Collegebound* and make it a beneficial resource for Christian parents. It's my prayer that God will greatly use this tool for His Glory and Kingdom!

Introduction

It seems like yesterday that our children were toddlers, taking their first steps, learning what "NO" means, and speaking their first words. It's hard to believe these same children are nearing their college years. We've strived to provide for them, given them opportunities to try a lot of things, encouraged and empowered them in their areas of strength, and most important, strived to shape them into godly young adults. In other words, we've been shepherding their hearts, much like Christ modeled during His earthly ministry.

Well, a great opportunity lies before us as parents—the opportunity to partner with our children in choosing a college. You are not alone in your interest in being a part of this all-important decision. Parents are becoming more involved in this process of transitioning their children out of their direct oversight into colleges and universities. Authors Neil Howe and William Strauss, in their books *Millennials Rising* and

Millennials Go to College, document the characteristics of today's young people and the phenomenon of parents hovering over their children. We are interested in being engaged in the lives of our kids; however, many of us struggle with the process as our kids grow older. Not only is it difficult to know *what* to do, but *how* to do it with often-temperamental teens! Yes, being involved is a challenge, but I can assure you it's worth the effort. This book is all about you being part of the process and knowing the facts, so that you and your teen can make a wise choice.

I approach this book as a fellow parent about to embark on the same process as you. My wife, Carolyn, and I have four teenagers who will enter into college in the next few years. However, I also approach this book with a great deal of passion as this topic represents the majority of my professional life's service in the areas of admissions, retention, financial aid, and student services at three different institutions. In my own educational background, I studied at a number of types of institutions, including a community college, two Bible colleges, and a research university. My degrees have been focused on educational practice, college student personnel, as well as educational administration and policy studies.

The convergence of my roles as parent, higher-education professional, and author, not to mention the convictions I bring as a believer in Christ, led me to write this book. My calling from God has been to serve in Christian higher education, and this book is an outgrowth of that inner conviction. My goal is to inform and encourage the parents of college-bound students to not only know what to do, but more important to also see this period of their lives as a unique opportunity to mentor and guide their children. As I read recently, the word *parent* is a verb as well as a noun. It's more than just a title for parents to hold—it requires action.

In my experience, the hands-off approach to parenting teenagers generally leads to undesirable outcomes. Staying engaged in parenting takes more effort and may generate more challenges with your teens along the way, but it pays off. There's a lot at stake with where your teens end up at college—and you want to make sure you do everything you can to help them flourish academically, emotionally, physically, and most of all spiritually. Making sure they are in an environment where they can grow in their walk with Christ is important. You don't want to see them flounder in their faith—or take an out-of-control tailspin.

Thinking back to when your kids were small, what were your hopes and aspirations for them? Any dreams of splendor come to mind? Well, you're not unusual to have thought that way. When our third child, Cathy, was born, she had multiple abnormalities and therefore was in the neonatal intensive care unit for nine days. Over one hundred tests were conducted on her while she was hanging on to life. Besides praying for healing of whatever was wrong, one of our prayers for Cathy was that she would be a fighter and not give up. Well, God answered our prayers, and she is a bright and healthy teen today. The doctors called her recovery a diagnostic dilemma—we prefer to call it a miracle of God. And yes, by the way, she is a fighter, undaunted by any foe, especially on the basketball court. Our dreams for her and the other children, while unique, are a joy to us.

When it comes to college, are you predisposed to a certain one? There are some parents who have predetermined college choices, even before their babies can walk! You know who they are. They're the parents dressing their toddlers in their favorite college's T-shirt with print that says "Class of 2022"! Or they're the ones who brag about prepaying tuition at today's rate for their children who will enroll at "their college" fourteen years from now. Parents who do this tend to either be extremely loyal alumni of their alma maters, fans of their sports teams, live in the area, or have a strong need to control their kids.

Since I grew up in Ohio and spent eleven years in Tennessee, believe me, I've been around people who are loyal to their state universities. As someone who works in higher education, I find that there's something assuring about that level of appreciation, loyalty, and support from constituents. However, as it relates to choosing a college or university, we should want what's best for our kids—not what we as parents are predisposed to liking. That kind of certainty alarms me. While I've known a lot of knowledgeable and wise parents, I haven't met any who can claim omniscience. Choosing a college without input from your child, let alone claiming you have God's will on the matter, is a bit pretentious. It may sound outrageous that parents would actually think this way, but believe me—it's true.

Even if you fall into the category of those parents having strong loyalties to a particular college or university, think about what is best for your kids. You certainly should present your preferred college to them, but make sure there are other options for them to consider that meet your and their criteria. Just as you don't want to leave the search totally up to your child, neither should you push one college too hard. Neither extreme works well.

And keep in mind that each child is unique and will not

necessarily want the same college experience as you—or their sibling(s). Children, as God's unique creations, need our assistance to explore and narrow down the options before deciding which college is the best fit.

The college search is as much an *art* as it is a science. The *science* of it is well documented through years of work researchers and practitioners have invested in studying this phenomenon. This book highlights the typical benchmarks, as well as features all the major points of the process to demystify what can be an intimidating endeavor for parents and students.

The *art* part of the college search has to do with all the unique aspects of this process. The added dimension that this book encompasses is the role and involvement of Christian parents who are desirous of helping their children find the best college or university to flourish not only academically, but also spiritually. This way they will be well prepared for the world with a solid, biblical worldview when they graduate from college.

When you combine both the *art* and *science* of choosing a college or university, it's a journey that you'll never forget. It's kind of exciting (and maybe scary) to be thinking about narrowing the almost 4,200 United States degree-granting college possibilities down to one, isn't it? Don't panic though, *Collegebound* will walk you through the process.

1

Knowing Your Role and Your Student

Every fall in the United States, nearly three million students embark on their final year of high school.[1] They bask so briefly in the satisfaction that their final year of secondary education is nearly completed. Whether they spend that year at a military academy, home school, boarding school, Christian or public school, they are the shining stars and hometown heroes. Some of them hold positions in the spotlight like quarterback of the football team, prom queen, debate champion, or youth group president. Others are unofficial leaders of their millennial generation and set fashion trends, serve as comedians, or talk a techno-game language distinguishable only to those in-the-know and aspiring wannabes.

Then, without notice, these surreal seniors morph into panic-stricken, paralyzed, prospective college students.

What triggers such a dramatic change in demeanor? Out of the blue, between classes at school or church services, a friend innocently raises the question, "Where are you going to college?" The words pierce the psyche, not because the idea of progressing from high school to college is anything new, but because this student has been living in the present—wrapped up in studying, community service, youth group, and/or a part-time job. The idea of the college search kept getting pushed back on the agenda because it seemed to be *way off* in the future. But the question is still hanging out there: "Where are you going to college?" Most of our kids will be able to come up with the name of their dream college and an alternative or two with some kind of response like, "Yes, I'm looking into the Naval Academy if I can get my congressman to recommend me, or if that doesn't work out, I've often wondered about places like Baylor, UCLA, Wheaton, or UMass . . ." But as the senior year progresses, panic can set in.

It's okay for a student to be undecided about college and admit, "I'm not sure which college yet, but that's something I sure need to pray about and get busy doing." The most important thing is to transfer the energy that could be spent in stressed-out mode and reinvesting it in productive college search activities.

A question many parents ask is, "How can I help my teenager engage in thinking about the college choice without adding stress to his life?" Well, if nothing is happening, then do something—anything—to get the process started. "But wait a minute," you say, "where do we start?" Take a deep breath, relax, and read on. You've already jumped in by picking up this book that will walk you through the process.

You do have a lot to offer along the way, and you can be instrumental in the college decision. "Pardon me, though," you may retort, "you don't know my teenager! He isn't exactly asking for my advice." The key is to avoid stepping in to decide for him. As you've probably discovered, that doesn't go over very well with teenagers. You need to be helpful but not overbearing. Certainly, you don't want to sour his remaining time under your roof, let alone your long-term relationship. Walk beside him through this time because it's one of your last significant opportunities to help him chart the course for his future. You'll be pleased to know that *it is possible* to be involved in the college search process without being a pain in the neck! In speaking of parents' tendencies to be tentative with their teens, author Tedd Tripp commented:

> Many parents disengage. They give up on the idea of being a nurturing influence in the life of their teen. . . . All the issues that require parental correction, direction and involvement are opportunities for understanding and embracing our teens. . . . All the hopes, fears, aspirations, questions, doubts, goals and dreams of our teens are opportunities to shepherd their hearts.[2]

A few years back, a friend of mine named Paul was apprehensive about recommending a local college that was a possible fit for one of his sons, Dave (not actual names). Paul hoped that Dave would come to this realization on his own. This school offered a quality academic program with a thoroughly integrated biblical worldview, plus a small faculty-to-student ratio and opportunities for ministry throughout the community. It made total sense to him as a dad. However, Paul didn't want to pressure his son, so he backed off from encouraging him in this direction, choosing instead to let Dave make his own choice—hoping it would be the local college. Well, Dave made his choice, and it wasn't that college. He enrolled at a well-known university, flourished academically, but starved spiritually. For whatever reasons, Dave didn't get connected with campus ministry organizations or a local church, but instead got caught up in his studies and university life. Those four years prepared him for making a living, but not for the really important things in life. Dave graduated and is doing well for himself but not living for God. Paul now regrets acquiescing his involvement in this decision. He loves him dearly and is proud of his son, but wonders "what if" he had been more involved at a strategic point in Dave's life.

So how do you capture the balance of having a godly influence on the college decision with minimal discomfort, while preserving the child's interest in looking around and dreaming big dreams? The simple, and most meaningful, answer to that question is found in the Bible.

A BIBLICAL PERSPECTIVE FOR PARENTS

Scripture has a lot to say about parents shepherding the hearts of their children, and it certainly applies to staying engaged in their lives amidst the college search. Moses described a central part of our role in Deuteronomy 6:6–9:

> *These commandments that I give you today are to be upon your hearts. Impress them on your children. Talk about them*

when you sit at home and when you walk along the road,
when you lie down and when you get up. Tie them as symbols
on your hands and bind them on your foreheads. Write them
on the doorframes of your houses and on your gates.

The expectation is that we are responsible to be actively involved in the development of our children's hearts—and to continually espouse God's Word in relevant ways. Earlier in Deuteronomy chapter 4 verse 9, we are encouraged to pass God's commands on—not only to our children, but also our grandchildren! That's a long-range view on parenting, isn't it? These Old Testament passages emphasize being with your kids, spending time with them, and being attentive to their needs. It means taking the everyday circumstances they are encountering and applying biblical truth to them. Notice that in chapter 6 of Deuteronomy, verses 8–9 acknowledge that we need to make God's commands obvious.

Many of our kids today are visual in how they learn, and Moses shares that God's Word needs to surround them. In today's culture, youth have opportunities to have their hearts and minds stimulated by artwork, prose, story, and music that aligns with the Christian worldview. And it goes without saying that they need to be immersed in relationships with other Christian teenagers to help support and encourage their faith.

This brings me to a critical point. Your teen's foundation of faith should be a strong consideration when choosing a college. During those undergraduate years, he will learn not only *what* to think, but *how* to think. Your student will question many things during college, including his faith. And the questioning of faith is not necessarily a bad thing—it's a normal part of development. Think of it as an *unpacking of faith.* By

examining the validity of his belief in God against other systems (religious and philosophical) through Scripture and other
extrabiblical evidence, hopefully he will be able to *repack the
faith*. And, by the way, going through this process does in fact
lead to *ownership of the faith.*

It's important to keep in mind that there are risks at any
college—but especially at secular institutions. Respected higher education researcher Alexander Astin found that there were
decreases in religious behaviors at public and selective, prestigious, nonreligious colleges and universities.[3] In fact, a research study by Gary Railsback a decade ago found that 34
percent of all students who entered a public university claiming to be "born again" no longer held to their faith upon graduation. He also discovered an additional 28 percent of
self-proclaimed Christian students, who, upon completion at a
public university, had not attended a church or religious service in the previous year.[4] If you combine those two percentages, 52 percent deliberately or subtly stepped away from their
faith.

Did you get that? That startling statistic predicts that one
out of two of our kids at secular colleges and universities will
discard their faith by the time they finish their undergraduate
degree.

A more recent study by Steve Henderson confirmed the
negative effect that non-Christ-centered colleges and universities have on Christian students. In particular, his research
showed that independent colleges, state universities, Presbyterian colleges, and Catholic institutions were most detrimen-
tal to students' faith. This outcome reveals not only that these
are difficult places for Christian students, but also the subtle
difference between some institutions with a religious heritage

and Christ-centered colleges and universities (those holding membership in the Council for Christian Colleges and Universities [CCCU] or the North American Coalition for Christian Admissions Professionals [NACCAP]). Henderson stated, "The affiliation of the college does appear to make a difference in the overall change in religiosity."[5]

You may be asking, "Okay, when does the commercial start for distinctively Christian colleges?" The fact of the matter is that there are no colleges, secular or Christian, that can claim to be foolproof in preserving faith. This is why it is important to know your student, be involved in his life, and be knowledgeable about the distinctives of the various college options to help him find the best fit—so he has the best environment to not only spiritually survive, but flourish.

But you need to know that I'd be remiss if evangelical, Christ-centered colleges and universities weren't mentioned at this point because of their spiritually charged environment to make Christian growth easier. Most students *do* thrive in their faith in these environments. The earlier mentioned Henderson study confirmed this spiritual growth factor by stating, "Students who attend CCCU or NACCAP related institutions showed significant positive differences on almost all individual measures of religiosity as well as overall changes in religiosity compared to those who attended non-member institutions."[6]

However, spiritual growth is *not* a given in spite of the environmental influences toward Christianity. While their struggle is not as pervasive as that of their secular university peers, some students on Christian campuses have difficulty assimilating their faith. The Railsback study showed that 6 percent of Christian kids at evangelical Christian colleges (CCCU member institutions) walked away from their faith.[7] While this is a

lower number, it does illustrate the fact that students struggle
to some degree with their faith, regardless of the campus.

You may be asking, "Is there reason for hope that my child
could survive in a public/nonreligious institution?" The answer is YES. There are thousands of committed Christians at
these universities growing in their faith in spite of the antagonism they encounter daily in their classes as well as in the residence halls and fraternities/sororities. Strong Christian young
people are needed to share the good news of the gospel.

What are the keys for your student to find success in her
faith if she enrolls at a secular campus? University of Texas-
Austin professor J. Budziszewski, in his book *How to Stay
Christian in College: An Interactive Guide to Keeping the Faith*,
says:

> Keep up your spiritual disciplines. What I mean by that is
> daily prayer, frequent Bible study and worship, evangelism,
> service to others, and constantly reminding yourself of the
> presence of God. If you stay focused on Christ, He'll make
> even a desert bloom.[8]

He goes on in the book to share the importance of having
partners in the faith and having fellowship. I agree whole-
heartedly— believing that students in a secular context must
have a close group of Christian friends, either that they know
from home or through building new relationships at the university. It goes without saying that the core group of friends in
college determines to a large degree a person's college experience—and much of whom someone becomes during that period of time commonly carries over into adult life. Finding
fellowship in campus ministries such as InterVarsity, Campus

Crusade, Navigators, or Fellowship of Christian Athletes (FCA) is essential. Students, regardless of the type of college they attend, also need to find a good evangelical church in town that serves students seeking worship, Bible teaching, fellowship, and ministry opportunities. It is God's plan for believers to be a part of "the church" in a universal sense, as well as on a local level. Of course, students who don't place themselves in these friendships, churches, or campus ministry organizations won't have positive support systems for spiritual growth, and therefore their faith will be vulnerable.

As a shepherd figure, you need to help provide, protect, correct, advise, and direct. In the book of John, Jesus describes this role of shepherd.

> *I am the good shepherd. The good shepherd lays down his life for the sheep. The hired hand is not the shepherd who owns the sheep. So when he sees the wolf coming, he abandons the sheep and runs away. Then the wolf attacks the flock and scatters it. The man runs away because he is a hired hand and cares nothing for the sheep. I am the good shepherd; I know my sheep and my sheep know me.* (10:11–14)

Certainly, of all people, you as parent-shepherd should be in the best position to know your student, care for him, and help determine what is best for him in the future. You are not a hired hand—you give wise counsel out of love. But, when you think about it, whom do we tend to rely on in advising our children regarding college choice? It's the professionals— the guidance counselor at school or the youth pastor at church. While people serving in these positions are typically well trained and well intentioned (and we do need to use their expertise), they don't have the understanding of your teen that you have . . . or the depth of your love. With that in mind, don't outsource your responsibility as a parent-shepherd. Take advantage of these professionals' expertise, advice, and ideas, but don't rely solely on them—*stay engaged.*

We usually think about nurturing our children's hearts when they are in the more pliable primary years. It's true that when they are younger they absorb a lot (usually without a lot of resistance). But as time goes on, we as parents change, and without doubt our teenagers change. They're developing into young adults, while we as parents get so involved with other responsibilities that we neglect to give them the degree of time and attention they need. It reminds me of a telephone service box found on the side of a road near our home. My wife, Carolyn, and I recently noticed it being repaired by a telephone company technician in our neighborhood. As we looked inside the box, we were amazed at the thousands of colored wires filling the space—and that the intricate wiring all made sense when it came time to make a phone call or receive a fax. Sometimes the complexity of our daily lives doesn't always allow for immediate connections of the heart to occur with our teenagers. Yet, the master technician is God. He is the one who helps us keep connections strong and clear with the hearts of those that He intricately designed.

Through His Word and our effective, fervent prayers to Him—we have access to wisdom beyond our knowledge or experience. Our dependence on Him and passion for growing spiritually will fuel the fire that helps us develop into more mature believers and give us something of significance to pass on to our kids in their adolescent years. Joshua 1:8 provides the rationale for this type of spiritual discipline.

*Do not let this Book of the Law depart from your mouth;
meditate on it day and night, so that you may be careful to do
everything written in it. Then you will be prosperous and
successful.*

So what we're looking at is a mature stage of nurturing. A development of the heart that allows for interaction between us and our teenagers involving mutual respect (including being able to admit when we're wrong and asking for forgiveness), communication (listening as well as talking), integration of relevant truth from the Bible, affirmation, and expression of love. It all boils down to a good relationship with our children and a realization that because of this, we have an opportunity to help guide them in a positive direction in making a college decision. If there are issues and unresolved differences between you and your teens, seek to resolve them first. They need our godly counsel.

READINESS FACTOR

The readiness of your child for higher education is an important consideration when assessing which college is best for your child. Our children mature and develop at different paces, and while society may say that after high school they need to go to college right away, that advice may be the worst thing for them to follow.

While recruiting a student out of eastern Pennsylvania in the mid-1990s, I was impressed with his vision, his love for Christ and energy for serving Him, as well as his academic background. He was a perfect fit for the college where I was serving at the time—Bryan College in Dayton, Tennessee.

However, his parents thought he needed more time to grow and mature before starting a four-year undergraduate degree. He agreed with their counsel and arranged to have his admission to college deferred for a year. He took that year to tour with a Youth for Christ (YFC) musical group. It was a great experience that allowed him to see a lot of the United States and taught him about himself and others, as well as the price and demands of serving people. After that year with YFC, he came to college with a lot more maturity, more certainty about his goals, and a better preparation to tackle the demands of higher education. He excelled and went on to work on a master's degree in music technology in Nashville.

Sometimes taking a year off before college as he did can be a wise choice. Considering that 32.7 percent of freshmen nationwide will not return to the same college the following year as sophomores (for a variety of reasons), should cause you to question if your child will be ready to adjust and succeed.[9] This is especially true if your child is undecided about his major/career interest, is academically underprepared, or lacks motivation. The cost of college is too high for most parents to warrant a high-risk venture. It's not good for the student, or for the institution, if your child has a bad experience.

If your student knows his college major or desired career field, it typically leads to a higher level of motivation and persistence. If that clarity for future direction is not present, motivation levels can fluctuate, especially if your student's academic history isn't especially strong. It's okay to delay the start of college in order to gain a stronger sense of God's direction and to grow in Him. But many parents are fearful of delaying college because of what other people will think, the effect of their child working and getting accustomed to a paycheck, or the possible ill effects of their child sitting around and doing nothing. But there are some productive—even valuable things—your child can do if he doesn't go to college right away.

A number of possibilities are available for that period of time when your children are deciding future direction. Just a few of these options include short-term missions, traveling music groups, sports ministry traveling teams, military service, apprentice work, and Christian camps. Some of the best Christian camps/programs are through Torchbearers' Schools (www.capernwray.org.uk), Word of Life Bible Institute (www.wol.org/biblei), and Summit Ministries summer conferences, which offer two-week summer programs in Colorado, Tennessee, and Ohio that are specifically designed to help Christian students prepare for post-Christian culture as experienced on college campuses. Your children will grow and mature tremendously during these experiences and be much better equipped for college later on. While not for everyone, these kinds of experiences tend to fortify the degree of certainty your child will have about the future and which type of college is best. And, if this time helps them determine that they really don't want to go to college, it's good to know that before putting them through an unnecessary struggle.

An Overview of the Process

The three major stages of college selection are *predisposition, search,* and *choice* as noted by Hossler and Gallagher.[1] The *predispositional* stage is the period of time in which students and their parents determine if college is the right option for them. In today's American society it is widely accepted that just about all high school graduates will pursue higher education. While that is assumed, it is important to pause and carefully consider if your student *should* go to college. I believe there are some commonsense factors to think about in determining this. Some questions you need to ask yourself are:

- Has your student shown evidence of being able to handle the rigor of academic life?
- Does she tend to be persistent in following through on projects and assignments in school?

- Does she have interests outside of reading, writing, and studying?
- What kind of thinker is she? Concrete (more practical) or abstract (more theoretical)?

It goes without saying that high ability, motivated students have a high probability for college success. Conversely, students who lack either motivation or ability have lower likelihood for success in college.

Choosing to forgo college and do something else does not mean your child will not be a valuable, contributing member of society. There are many successful, contented, happy people who never went to college. Many of them are the bedrock of our communities, providing the stability and security needed to provide a high quality of life for families. Also, just because someone doesn't go to college right away doesn't disqualify her going in the future. It's becoming increasingly common for older adults to attend college.

When thinking about the *predisposition* stage, it's interesting to note the degree to which parents influence the college decision:

> Parents' expectations and encouragement have the greatest effect on the predisposition stage of the college decision-making process. This is followed by student achievement, parents' educational level, the influence of peers, and involvement of students in high school organizations and activities.[2]

So you can see that parents are an integral part of the college choice decision right from the start. It's important for you to talk with your teens about college and help them determine if they should pursue higher education after their high school studies. If that answer is yes, it's time to move on to the next stage.

The *search* stage involves sorting through the various college options. Although the thought of looking at 4,168 colleges is intimidating, the search itself doesn't need to be. Once criteria of what students want and need are established, this knowledge lays the basis for broad classifications of identifying schools that match. For example, if your teen wants to stay in state, major in political science, and play percussion in a marching band—the options quickly narrow to a handful of colleges or universities. With this example, you can see how quickly your top schools will emerge. On the other hand, if she wants to major in business, work on the school newspaper, and be involved in community service at a small private college, the choices abound. Hundreds of colleges will match those criteria. Secondary factors may need to be established to drill down deeper into what would be the best fit for your child. Preferences like denomination background, size and ethnic makeup of the student body, cost of attendance, as well as the school's reputation might need to come into play.

And, as you've probably already discovered, the *search* stage is not a set period of time. It can vary from a few weeks to a few years. A lot depends on when you start the process and how soon the enrollment date is approaching. During this time, families should use the suggestions found in chapter 3 for sources and means of requesting information about the various schools.

Along the way in the *search* stage, I'd encourage your family to keep an open mind about colleges you've never heard of before. Given my interest in higher education, I enjoy visiting college campuses as I travel around the country. It's fascinating to learn of the history and distinctives of some of the lesser known but significant institutions that dot the countryside. Places like Fisk University in Nashville, Wilson College in Pennsylvania, Metropolitan State College in Denver, Eureka College in Illinois, and Southwestern College in Phoenix all offer quality programs without a lot of hoopla. Just remember that in our age of *bigger is better,* the educational quality of institutions isn't determined by the number of members of the basketball team that get drafted into the NBA. Nor is it ascertained by the size of their campus facilities or endowment. While large, well-resourced schools do offer a lot, keep in mind that some of the best institutions for delivering quality undergraduate education are small- to medium-sized institutions that just focus on the main thing—educating and developing students.

The *choice* stage takes place as students make final considerations of colleges that meet their criteria during the *search* stage. Carefully reviewing the brochures, websites, and CD-ROMs that your family has access to will guide you to which campuses to visit. During this evaluative process, schools will be actively recruiting your teen by phone and e-mail. These encounters with admissions counselors, faculty, and current students can be a valuable source of information and a great way to get your questions answered. All colleges encourage campus visits, so you'll want to make that a priority during the *choice* stage. Chapter 6 provides detail about how you can make the most of these visits.

During the *choice* stage, the next natural progression in choosing a college is your student applying for admission to her top colleges and universities. And, yes, it is acceptable to apply to multiple colleges. In fact, many students apply to at least three schools that meet their criteria. Doing so allows them a chance to take a closer look at each and compare and contrast their options. Being in the applicant cycle also places your student in the position to be considered for institutional scholarships and grants. Given that the final cost for college is a factor for most parents, the financial aid awarding process requires students to be applicants and in some cases accepted freshmen. An additional benefit for your teenager being an applicant is the closer communication ties such a status affords with admissions counselors and other key college personnel such as faculty members and student development staff. The interaction and information they provide will assist you in making a wise college choice.

In considering your potential influence in these three stages, Hossler, Braxton, and Coopersmith (1989) found in a study that parental encouragement has the largest impact during the *predisposition* and *search* stages, when parameters such as net cost and distance from home are being set.[3] They also found parental influence at the *choice* stage was active, but not as great as earlier stages. J. Blair Blackburn found a similar outcome in a more recent study with students and parents in Texas.[4] My encouragement is that you stay engaged with your child throughout the journey of the various stages. You don't want to become complacent toward the end of the college decision.

TIMELINE

Students are considering colleges earlier in high school than ever before. The search is on, especially for highly motivated students who have strong direction. Students taking assessment tests in their sophomore year such as the PSAT and ACT PLAN, many times hear from colleges who notice their good initial scores. It's also not unusual for admissions offices at colleges and universities to receive inquiries from students in their freshman year of high school. While these institutions are usually happy to make information available to underclassmen, they spend the majority of their time and attention with juniors and seniors.

Most collegebound students begin the process late in their sophomore year and get more serious about the college search through the junior year. By starting fairly early, families can investigate standards for admission at some of their top schools and still have time to respond to unanticipated requirements. For instance, some colleges will expect certain subjects to be taken in high school, or others may require a certain exposure to foreign language, community service participation, or leadership experience. By knowing these kinds of things, parents can help their teens arrange those experiences before the colleges begin evaluating their admission files.

The junior year of high school is really the time to get active in the college search process. For most collegebound students, I recommend they take the ACT and the SAT during junior year to get accustomed to the format of each and to get an initial assessment of their scores. Given that these tests can be retaken (recommended), the outcome of the test isn't terribly important at this point unless the student is applying for the National Merit Scholarship Program competition (www. nationalmerit.org). The majority of students will find that the additional study that goes into their junior and senior year classes will give them the ability to improve their scores, which plays into admission and institutional scholarship offers later on.

The junior year of high school is also a great time to visit the campuses of the top colleges that fit the students' criteria. The most comprehensive and useful visits will take place during the school year when classes are in session. Some people like to attend the "visit events" that colleges and universities offer, while others like to check things out on a normal college day. Both are useful. However, with that said, if you're just starting to look at various college options, consider planning summer vacations around campus visits to get a general idea of what each college has to offer. Even though classes aren't in session, these vacation trips help answer some of the general questions about colleges and make it clear if certain ones should be considered further.

The senior year tends to focus more on taking final standardized college entrance tests (ACT/SAT), filing applications, writing essays, and applying for scholarships/financial aid. While not as exciting as traveling around looking at campuses, it is a time to prayerfully consider the options, asking God for His clarity on which institution to choose. If it takes another campus visit to a couple of your top schools, or a few phone calls to alumni in your area, or a chat session with current students to help you make your final choice—by all means take advantage of those opportunities. For most families, the period of time in the spring is dedicated to applying for financial aid and scholarships to their top schools culminating in a decision by May 1. More details about the admissions and financial aid process are included in chapters 7 and 9.

The timeline as it has been described is in a general form. It's important to realize that the many events that surround and lead up to the ultimate college selection are flexible to a large degree and dependent on you and your student. A case in point was a college visit that I took with my son to visit Cedarville University in Ohio. Andrew was in the fall of his sophomore year of high school at the time, but because I was attending an event for work on the Cedarville campus, it was an ideal time to take him along with me. He had a good visit, and it gave him an idea of what college is like and a basis for which to compare other college options that we will consider in the future. Of course, other families will wait until the senior year of high school before starting to think about college and then engage in a much more abbreviated schedule of college search activities.

The bottom line is that the college search experience can be a time of panic or an exciting faith venture. Proverbs 3:5–6 serves as a reminder for us:

"Trust in the LORD with all your heart and lean not on your own understanding; in all your ways acknowledge him, and he will make your paths straight."

Before you progress deeper into this book, take a few moments to commit this college search experience to the Lord. As you depend on Him, rest assured that He will direct you and your child to make a wise choice.

WHAT ARE COLLEGES LOOKING FOR?

Ahh . . . the age-old question. *"What are the factors that influence colleges and universities to determine which students to admit?"* In a recent survey of admissions officers by the National Association for College Admission Counseling (NACAC), a number of factors were rated as to the degree they influenced admission decisions. Below are the results of the NACAC

2003–2004 State of College Admission Report showing the
moderate to considerable roles these factors play.[5]

Factor	Considerable Influence	Moderate Influence
Grades in college-prep courses	78%	11%
Standardized admissions tests	61%	25%
Grades in all courses	54%	31%
Class rank	33%	35%
Essay or writing sample	23%	35%
Counselor recommendation	17%	42%
Teacher recommendation	18%	39%
Work and extracurricular activities	7%	40%
Interview	9%	27%
Student's demonstrated interest	7%	23%
Subject tests (SAT II, AP, IB)	7%	18%
State graduation exam scores	7%	11%
Race/ethnicity	3%	16%
Ability to pay	2%	6%
State or county of residence	2%	6%

These percentages give you a glimpse into what is considered important in the eyes of admissions officers. While these
percentages may not surprise you, they serve as affirmation of
what counts in getting into colleges.

3

The World of College Possibilities

The number of degree-granting higher education institutions in the United States is 4,168.[1] That's a lot of options! However, when you start narrowing down the characteristics of the various distinctions of colleges and universities, the number of viable choices becomes a little more manageable. The broadest categories are public (1,712) and private (2,456) institutions. Public institutions enroll approximately 11.5 million students each year, while private institutions have approximately 3.5 million enrollees. Chapter 4 provides an indepth look at the most popular college and university types that offer undergraduate education.

Beyond the private and public designation, there are many

other ways to categorize and sort colleges and universities. Some of these distinctions include size, location, denomination, history, majors, and extracurricular activities (sports, music groups, publications, and Greek life). Some institutions are highly specialized—for example, women's colleges. There are fifty-seven such institutions in the United States enrolling 93,430 women students.[2] They are distinctive in having a history of enrolling only women, and because of that, are able to focus on them and address issues that coed institutions cannot touch.

Patrick Henry College in Virginia, founded in 2000, caters to home-educated graduates. Other examples of unique institutions include the over one hundred historically black colleges and universities, as well as military academies such as West Point, the Naval Academy, and the Air Force Academy.

There are also unique colleges that offer special majors by virtue of their founder's vision or their location. For example, Houghton College in rural western New York offers a program in equestrian studies, which provides a great place for students to study, ride, and work with horses in a farmlike atmosphere. Berea College in Kentucky has a unique mission in that they serve underprivileged youth in Appalachia. In exchange for fulfilling responsibilities in a mandatory work program, they provide their students with free tuition. Many of their majors relate to occupations designed to prepare students to meet the needs of the Appalachian region of the South. In the Rocky Mountains, the University of Montana offers four undergraduate majors related to forestry and conservation to prepare students to meet the needs of a state widely known for its natural resources. Bryan College in Tennessee provides a political science and government studies program because of the legacy of the school's founder, William Jennings Bryan. Mr. Bryan was a United States senator, Secretary of State, and a three-time candidate for president. Dwight Lyman Moody founded Moody Bible Institute to train young people for ministry. Even after 120 years, all the majors at this Bible college are linked to this original intent.

THE NEW COLLEGE "COURTSHIP"

I don't know about you, but looking back on my college search experience, my options were fairly limited. Not because there weren't enough colleges or universities in existence at that time—but because I had little exposure. In the late '70s and '80s when my friends and I were searching for schools during our high school years, there wasn't a tremendous amount of resources to assist us. As you'll see later in this chapter, a multitude of college search tools are available to us these days, which allow us to assist our collegebound children.

Today, marketing efforts have evolved into highly sophisticated techniques founded on proven business intelligence models and market research, helping the colleges target which students would be a good fit for them. This approach allows schools to better allocate their marketing resources, as well as leverage financial aid to make enrollment more probable for those targeted students.

This way of marketing is efficient and effective for institutions. It is also good for families, since the schools aren't just looking for warm bodies to fill the dorms and classrooms, regardless of a good match. Having the wrong students enroll, then depart after a semester or two, is not a good scenario.

You may be asking, "If colleges are targeting more, why

hasn't that impacted the amount of mail we receive from them?" Well, primarily because more and more colleges each year are taking part in advanced marketing methods, which increases the amount of mail/e-mail that gets sent to college-bound students. But don't fret. Institutions that send you those initial mailings typically do so only once. If you like what you see and respond for more information, they will place your child in their computer database for future contacts. If you don't respond after those initial mailings, they usually won't pursue your child further.

Of course, you can contact colleges and universities on your own and they will gladly send information about their offerings, as well as details related to their admissions process. By the way, if after receiving information from a college, you realize it is not a good fit for your child, just contact their admissions office and ask to be taken off their mailing list. They'll be happy to do this because they don't want to irritate you, plus it will be a benefit to them by saving money in printing and postage costs.

Fortunately for many of us who are parents of college-bound students, we benefit from marketing sophistication, not to mention advances in computer technology. We find out about more college and university options that could be a fit, which is a real blessing. We aren't limited to our own scope of known colleges and universities.

Internet and digital technology makes colleges on the other side of the country as accessible as those around the corner. Much of the technology that drives the information into your home was developed not so much by the colleges but by entrepreneurial companies that have sprung up to take the information to your student. Of course, colleges pay for involvement with those companies, which usually keeps the student from having to pay for accessing the information.

Therefore, be cautious of companies that charge for helping find a college or for assisting in obtaining scholarships. The types of services they are offering for a fee are usually available for free if you deal with the right companies or agencies. I don't want to smear all educational consultants who can help you with this process, because there are in fact some legitimate ones providing valuable services. Like most areas of business, it's unfortunate, but there are some swindlers out there taking advantage of families' gullibility, along with thousands of their dollars each year. Just be careful if you choose to hire private consultants. Word-of-mouth referrals are usually best in finding reputable assistance. You don't want to be ripped off, nor do you want to totally outsource your shepherding opportunity as a parent.

In regard to this flow of information that is streaming into our homes, keep in mind that it's our responsibility as parents to assure that we help our kids assimilate it in preparation for making a college choice. Invest some concerted time to help your children explore their possibilities. Even with all the college information coming in, it doesn't guarantee a wise choice. Too often, all the college mail gets stacked up in a pile on the student's desk in his room. Fully intending to look at it at some point, over time, the mountain of college envelopes filled with glossy brochures grows so tall that they never even get opened. I recommend that you set a time each week to sit down with your child and review what came in the mail during the week and sort through each envelope. Based upon your criteria (see chapter 5, "Criteria for Narrowing the Choices"), you and your student can eliminate some colleges that don't match what you're looking for and actually throw away those items. For example, if you're from Fairbanks, Alaska, and your son is not interested in leaving the state, anything received from outside of your geographic zone should be tossed. Or if his major is going to be accounting and he wants to play on the tennis team, some schools may not match both of those criteria. Make sure you help organize the mail from the colleges that do match his interests, so he can use that as a guide to know which schools to visit and eventually make application.

COLLEGE GUIDES

College guides have been a popular resource for parents and students for the past twenty years. They're the ones that you see in major bookstores that are about the size of phone books. These printed publications are typically released annually and include profiles on colleges as reported by the institutions themselves. They report similar categories of information so families can compare and contrast schools based on their criteria. They include an index, which allows you to find which schools offer certain majors and extracurricular activities. Many of them include postage-paid reply cards that you can fill out and return to let certain colleges know that you're interested. As the popularity of these guides have grown, the companies have begun segmenting the colleges into smaller categories such as four-year colleges, Christian colleges, two-year colleges, and in some cases, institutions within states. Examples of companies that produce these guides include the following:

Peterson's Guides

Barron's

Patterson's American Education Directory

Wintergreen Orchard House

Campus Life magazine College Guide (annual October issue)

US News & World Report America's Best Colleges (late August issue)

The printed editions have been a staple resource for years, and you'll find that some of them have websites that provide some of the same information. While college guides are very reliable sources of information, they do grow outdated quickly as colleges regularly change facts such as their majors, sports, costs, and financial aid.

WEB RESOURCES

The Internet is a great way to find colleges and drill down into details that are of interest to you. There are websites that assist you in searching for schools that match your criteria. They'll often provide links to colleges' websites for more detailed information. Some of these college search websites are:

www.christiancollegementor.org

www.xap.com

The companies offering these search services include hundreds of categories of information that are used as the basis for narrowing the search in a comparative way with other institutions.

However, sometimes you'll want to find information

about just one college that someone at work or church mentioned in passing. Some people try to guess the Web address of colleges and type them in, only to discover the result is the wrong institution. A lot of this occurs because of common college names or initials. For instance, there are multiple institutions called "Trinity," and not all of them can have the same Web address! Trinity International University is an evangelical institution that is headquartered in Deerfield, Illinois, with multiple campuses around the country (www.tiu.edu). Then there is Trinity University in Texas, a private institution that has a Presbyterian (USA) heritage, as well as Trinity Christian College, a Christian Reformed institution in Palos Heights, Illinois (www.trnty.edu). In Hartford, Connecticut, there is a private institution with Episcopalian roots named Trinity College (www.trincoll.edu), while in Florida there is a Bible college named Trinity College (www.trinitycollege.edu). On top of that, there's an online institution known as Trinity Bible College and Seminary, based out of Newburgh, Indiana (www.trinitysem.edu). If you type into your Web browser the address www.trinity.edu, you'll get the Texas institution. Is that confusing, or what?

When you encounter this and feel like you're lost, go into one of the popular search engines and type out the full name of the school (and the location if you know it). The school you're looking for and its link should be in the top ten results.

The benefit of Web resources is that colleges have the ability to keep their information up to date, so that you can be aware of the latest developments. However, the Web's greatest benefit is also its greatest liability. If colleges neglect their sites, they can be as out-of-date as printed college guides.

A great benefit of using the Internet to check out colleges

is that many offer immediate online response, via instant messaging, chat rooms, and good old-fashioned e-mail. Many schools offer a special inquiry form to use in requesting more information. It's good to use these because they give you all the categories of information that colleges need about your child so they can drop that data into their computer systems and send you the right brochures. Also, most colleges offer an online application so your student can just fill in the information on the computer, and then send it when he is ready. Most of these programs allow your student to come back multiple times to complete the application form, saving the latest version. When he is finished, he submits it and the colleges receive it almost immediately.

Some colleges and universities collaborate on their applications so that your child can fill out one form but have it sent to multiple institutions at the same time. One such program is called Common Application (www.commonapp.org); it is administered by the National Association of Secondary School Principals (NASSP). The program currently includes 255 participating colleges and universities that choose to use the same application forms. There are also commercial companies that provide this service, among them Xap (www.xap.com). Some states have partnered with Xap to provide statewide common applications. For instance, the California State University system uses this technology for all of its campuses. Of course, not all colleges you're considering may be a part of the network of participating institutions. So your student may still end up filling out multiple online forms if he is applying to several colleges.

Just a word about e-mail communication with colleges. I would encourage you to set up a separate e-mail account for your student to use just with colleges. It helps to keep the information flowing to one spot without cluttering up his normal e-mail address that he uses with friends. It also serves as a way to organize this part of his life.

The Internet has transformed the college search and choice process. Internet Resources starting on page 169 includes a summary of helpful websites listed throughout this book.

WORD OF MOUTH

Have you ever thought about how much credibility we place in endorsements from people we know and trust? Whether it's choosing a church, dentist, or florist, we rely on the experiences of others to help us make decisions. Don't underestimate the value of referrals from your friends and family members who have attended different colleges or have sent their kids to them. Based on their experiences, ask them specific questions about what a certain school was like—good and bad. Regardless of how loyal they are to the college, if they are a trusted friend or family member, they will give you the straight scoop. Even though they may not have liked a certain part of their experience at a college, it doesn't mean it will be a negative thing for your child. By virtue of their honesty in sharing a "not so great part" of their college years, it makes their sharing more credible.

Just recently, while talking with a fellow church member, Carolyn and I shared that our son, a high school junior, is considering engineering for a career. It turns out that his friend Ross from church is an engineer at Ispat Inland Steel Corporation in northwest Indiana. He told us about his alma mater, LeTourneau University in Texas, where he received his engineering education and training. Even though we've known of this university for years, having Ross's endorsement added value to this option. He also shared the names of other good engineering schools that we might want to consider. About the same time, I was talking with an academic colleague, Dr. Larry Mercer, who is on the board of trustees at LeTourneau and has a daughter enrolled there. He shared some additional insights about the university from the perspective of a board member, as well as the parent of a current student. These interactions were very helpful and added significant weight to the already good impression we had of LeTourneau.

So take the recommendations of family and friends to heart, as God may be using them to help steer you in a direction that you might not have considered before.

MAILBOX MYSTERY COLLEGES

Your teen returns from the mailbox with letters from colleges exclaiming, "Look, Mom and Dad, I got mail from three colleges today!" You've got to love watching that happen the first few weeks it occurs. High school students love mail and e-mail, and they seem to be affirmed by it. Their confidence appears to grow with each new mail delivery that includes them. They say, "Cool . . . all these colleges want me." However, the appeal of that does fade after a while, as the pile of unopened college packets grows, especially if the mailings are from schools that your teen has never heard of before. You may hear him saying things like "I wonder how they got my name . . ." and "Why would I want to go to a college that is single-gender?" Slowly, he begins losing interest—and may miss out on some excellent colleges that match his criteria.

Come to the rescue at this point and remind your student of the previously agreed-upon criteria. Assist him in rethinking the basic things he is looking for in the process. All of this can be very overwhelming to an adolescent. Some even panic, becoming paralyzed in moving ahead with the college search because it seems like so much so soon. Help him recognize the need to take this journey one day at a time, remembering Matthew 6:33–34.

But seek first his kingdom and his righteousness, and all these things will be given to you as well. Therefore do not worry about tomorrow, for tomorrow will worry about itself. Each day has enough trouble of its own.

Your godly counsel and care can help him realize that this process is manageable. You can also help him look at the information from the unfamiliar colleges, tossing out pamphlets from schools that aren't a match.

For some reason, we tend to think that if we haven't heard about a college or university before, that it can't be a good one. If you've ever moved to a new part of the country before, you know what it's like to come into contact with store chains and products that are unique to that area or region. When Carolyn and I moved to the Delaware Valley in Pennsylvania, we learned of Wawa Convenience Stores, Tastykakes, Herr's Potato Chips, and Strawbridge's department stores, just to name a few. Of course, many of the national brand names were competing there also. In many cases, once we learned of the quality and value of these regional brands, we were just as inclined to give them our business as the national brands. The same is true with colleges and universities that have more of a regional reputation. When we receive information from these mystery colleges, remember that they may be just as good as the national "name brand" institutions.

REQUESTING INFORMATION

Requesting information about colleges has never been easier because they, along with college search companies, provide user-friendly means of inquiring. But beware—taking the business reply response card out of the middle of one of the college guides, filling in the dots for each college advertiser, and sending it in will result in lots of mail and beautifully designed brochures. It adds up over time. A friend of ours in Tennessee actually weighed the amount of college mail they received for their daughter over the course of a couple of years, and I recall it weighing about one hundred pounds! If you don't mind the deluge of information and will take a look at all of it, I recommend that you open the door wide and say Aaahh! However, if you'd like to be a little more discriminating (and conserve a tree or two . . . or maybe a forest!), I recommend that you do some investigative research by reading the college ads and looking at their websites before inquiring. This will allow you to narrow down certain *types* of schools that fit. For instance, if you know your student wants ROTC, then check out that availability first with each institutional possibility. Or if you're a homeschool family, you may want to determine how "friendly" these colleges are to homeschool graduates who are being considered for admission and how well these students do in these environments.

As mentioned earlier, the Internet has made the process for inquiring about colleges very easy. If you like quick response or are short on time, definitely take advantage of this technology.

Colleges will generally require the following types of information when you inquire:

Name
Address
Phone number
E-mail address
Type/Name of high school (public, homeschool, private)
Year of high school graduation
Intended major/career interest
Extracurricular interests (sports, music, journalism, etc.)

Of course, don't feel awkward about picking up the phone and calling colleges to request information. The old-fashioned way (relational and low cost) of using their toll-free numbers gives you a chance to talk with someone and get some preliminary questions answered. You may bump up against some voicemail systems that are a bit irritating, but if you hang in there, you're usually given an option to talk to a human being! Ask to speak with an admissions counselor. These staff members are usually alumni of the college and are trained in working with prospective students and their parents.

4

Institutional Types

As mentioned previously, there are 4,168 degree-granting higher education institutions in the United States. These institutions are segmented into groups that represent uniqueness of ownership, control, governance, and/or affiliation. Even though some of these categorizations may make institutions look the same, you'll find differences when you look closer. For instance, universities that make up the Pac10 Conference are known, in a general sense, as institutions similar to one another. However, they span a geographic territory that spans from Washington state to as far south as Arizona. So while they are part of the same athletic conference, each university is quite unique. Or consider the Council for Christian Colleges and Universities (CCCU). It is made up of over one hundred seventy colleges and universities from all over the world and represents a wide range of evangelical denominations. So there is *likeness* as Christ-centered institutions, but not *sameness,* because of the distinctives of each campus. And it's the uniqueness of each campus, even within various groupings, that makes American higher education so valuable and sought after from people outside this country.

The *Chronicle of Higher Education* conducted a public opinion poll via telephone in February and March 2004 to determine how Americans felt about colleges and universities.[1] One of the questions asked was, "If money were not an issue, would you rather have your child attend a private or public university?" The results:

Private	47%
Public	22%
Doesn't matter	28%
Don't know	4%

Another question was, "Do you think in general the quality of education is better at private or public universities?" The results:

Better at private	46%
Better at public	13%
About the same	31%
Don't know	10%

Isn't it interesting that a relatively high percentage of people surveyed were apathetic about the choice between private and public institutions and which had better educational quality? There *are* differences between types, which need to be noted. If you can relate to the people who were a part of this research, I trust this chapter will help clarify the type of institution that might be a good fit for your teen(s).

A Non-Christian or Christian Emphasis?

One common factor in public (and many private) institutions is their non-Christian culture. Before we get into the categories of public and private schools, I'd like to mention a few things about non-Christian institutions that may be of assistance when considering the pros and cons of a college. This factor is worth emphasizing because it greatly affects the type of environment where your child will live.

While I have an appreciation for the role of public institutions (I am a graduate of a research university), and they all contribute to students' and the states' well-being, there are some potential liabilities for the Christian student. I'm not desirous of trashing non-Christian schools, because they may in fact be the best place for your student. However, too many parents have such a high confidence level in their state university that they don't feel there is a need to look further. They're content with the quality and scope of offerings, and they know the price is right. Another reason is convenience, because searching for other schools, admittedly, would take a lot more time and effort. In other words, it's the path of least resistance.

Many Christian parents naively send their student to a state school because of the affordable cost, without counting the cost of that experience on her spiritual well-being. In ten years, do you want to be asking yourself, "Was the cost really worth the price?" While some students are well suited for state schools and thrive, the fact is that not all Christian students are prepared for the environment of the public university. As parents, *you* have a responsibility to either prepare them, or send them to a college or university that will nurture their faith. To do otherwise is parental irresponsibility.

Some Christian parents assume that if their child goes to a non-Christian school and is involved in a Christian group on campus such as InterVarsity, Campus Crusade, Navigators, Baptist Student Union, or the Fellowship of Christian Athletes, that their college student will do fine in her Christian walk. While these are good organizations and they do significant ministry in evangelism outreach, discipleship, and community service, they fall short in one significant way. Their influence is disconnected from what is being postulated in the academic and social realms of the student's experience. In other words, the typical everyday experiences of your student will not include an integration of a Christian worldview. It's just not normative in public or secular universities. Paul's words in Colossians are relevant for Christians in today's public universities:

> *See to it that no one takes you captive through hollow and deceptive philosophy, which depends on human tradition and the basic principles of this world rather than on Christ.* (2:8)

Parents assume that with the separation of church and state, they can expect universities to be neutral toward their child's faith—not speaking for it or against it. Even in an age of pluralism and tolerance, when each individual's beliefs are supposed to be respected, the Christian student is rarely afforded that same level of respect in the classroom. And even if there was neutrality, does education really hold value apart from the truth found in God's Word? It's not unusual for

Christian students to register for a religion or Bible class at public and nonreligious universities with the hopes of that enriching their faith. How wrong they are. In *World* magazine, John Dawson writes that the church has not prepared young Christians for the liberal education programs at most universities. He writes, "Across the country, university and seminary students are being taught about the Bible by academics who doubt and often are antagonistic toward traditional teaching about what the Bible says and who Jesus Christ is."[2] Have you and your church done a good job preparing your child(ren) for a non-Christian culture?

Of course there are occasional exceptions to this attitude in public or nonreligious institutions, but overall an antagonistic perception has been cast over evangelicals because of our belief in absolute truth. Christians are commonly verbally berated when they write or orally espouse their faith or postulate a philosophical position based on faith. Therefore, in these environments our children's faith can slowly crumble into a pile of doubt, skepticism, and even unbelief.

Certainly some Christian students have a strong foundation in which to engage these difficult challenges of the secular college—and may God empower more of our Christian youth to positively influence these campuses for Christ. However, consider these dynamics carefully and ensure that your child will be able to build those bridges between Scripture and their academic content.

This sounds like a terrible commentary on our public and non-Christian universities, but that's a reality of academic life today. I have good friends on staff and faculty at these places. Some of them are believers who are faithful to the Lord and respected by their colleagues for their teaching and scholarship.

And, yes, while having to remain relatively quiet in their outward testimony, they are attempting to make a significant difference by being a light for Christ in some dark places.

You may feel like the public university is the right place and are asking, "How do I prepare my child for a secular institution?" Well, whether you know it or not—you have been. I believe that if your parenting has been centered on God's Word to help bring your children into a personal relationship with Him, as well as having helped them develop a biblical worldview by word and example, then a positive outcome is likely. Isaiah states:

> *As the rain and the snow come down from heaven, and do not return to it without watering the earth and making it bud and flourish, so that it yields seed for the sower and bread for the eater, so is my word that goes out from my mouth: It will not return to me empty, but will accomplish what I desire and achieve the purpose for which I sent it.* (55:10–11)

The training you've provided your children at home in the Word of God will not return void. Experiences such as involvement in your local church, community service, Christian camps, and missions trips all help reinforce biblical truth and teach young people how to be an example, even in a postmodern society.

If your collegebound teens don't have this strong faith foundation, you might want to think twice about sending them to a secular university right away. If they're on shaky ground and you're just not sure how they would do in a nonsupportive, even antagonistic environment, there are some special programs that you can take advantage of before college that can really give a boost to your child's preparedness. (See chapter 1 and the list of Internet resources starting on page 169 for more information.) Those programs do charge participation fees to attend, but consider them an investment—particularly if your student leaves better grounded in her faith. And you'll be saving money later if she ends up enrolling at a public school.

PUBLIC INSTITUTIONS

In highlighting institutional types, I've chosen to start with the public institution category. As the name suggests, these universities are owned, operated, and funded by the public and for the benefit of the public within individual states. They offer hundreds of majors, which make them very attractive in offering students specializations not available at smaller colleges and universities. Included in this broad category of institutions are 1,712 research universities, state universities, community colleges, and technology centers, which enroll 11.5 million students.[3]

Research Universities

These universities are typically the flagship institutions of each state and selective in admission to attract top students. They usually have different schools or colleges within the overall university structure (e.g., College of Business, College of Engineering, College of Education, College of Nursing). Research universities are among the best-known and best-resourced institutions as well—which makes them highly desirable to prospective students and therefore hard to get into.

A portion of their funding comes from state allocations as well as through special federal programs. Research is supported through corporations and governmental agencies, which also help contribute to an institution's overall financial well-being. The majority of these institutions also have high-profile athletic programs that generate revenue for the schools. In addition, private donations are raised from businesses and constituents of the universities such as alumni and athletic booster club members. Of course, parents and students generate dollars for the universities through the payment of tuition, room, board, and fees—in addition to the financial aid monies received through federal, state, local, and personal sources.

These research universities usually offer a full scope of programs including bachelor's, master's, and doctoral degrees. They are there to serve each state's public interests and needs. A number of these institutions also have land grant status, originating with the federal Morrill Act of 1862, which means that in exchange for land and financial resources, these schools serve the public interest by providing academic training in agriculture and mechanical arts curriculums. The government issued land grant status to additional public institutions in 1890 and 1994.

State Universities

These institutions also serve the public interest by offering a broad scope of programs including bachelor's, master's, and select doctoral programs. They have similar funding sources as the research universities, but they don't tend to be as high-profile and therefore don't regularly receive the same volume of dollars. Their admission standards are moderate and designed to attract quality students. They offer a broad spectrum of majors and many extra-curricular activities in the arts, athletics, and journalism. A number of these state universities also hold land-grant status. The American Association of State Colleges and Universities (AASCU) website provides a listing of these universities, which can be found at www.aascu.org.

Community Colleges

Many of these institutions were founded in the 1970s to broaden access to higher education by a larger portion of the population by offering associate degrees and certifications in career specializations. These colleges serve multiple groups of people, businesses, and community entities. You'll find students in their late teens and twenties who want to live at home for the first couple years after high school and earn an associates degree, and those who want to get their general education credits so they can transfer to a four-year college or university. You'll also find that community colleges are intended to serve adults who want to take classes and complete degrees to improve their standard of living or to meet their employer's training expectations. And there are people who just want to take some classes for fun in order to learn skills such as basic computer skills, glass cutting, or art. (My mother-in-law recently took a computer class and really enjoyed it!) The goal of community colleges is to make higher education available to the masses by being convenient, relevant, and affordable. In many states they also serve the technological training needs of local industries and businesses.

An emerging subset of community colleges is made up of tribal colleges. Since the 1970s, over thirty such institutions have been established which service the unique needs of American Indian populations. The American Indian Higher Education Consortium (AIHEC) serves as an agency for these institutions. The Equity in Educational Land-Grant Status Act of 1994 gave twenty-nine of these tribal colleges access to federal funding to enrich the offerings of these institutions. For more information about tribal higher education institutions go to: www.aihec.org.

To learn more about all community colleges and to search for institutions in your area you can go to www.aacc.nche.edu.

Technology Centers

In some states, technology centers provide post-secondary training in the skilled trades. Our teens can train for careers at these state-supported institutions in divisions such as electrical, plumbing, culinary, cosmetology, and auto mechanics, just to name a few. For example, in Wisconsin there are sixteen publicly operated technical colleges. They offer degrees, diplomas, and apprenticeships, plus they offer basic educational assistance to help students obtain high school diploma equivalency through GED.

MILITARY COLLEGES & SERVICE ACADEMIES

Military institutions are designed to educate students in a variety of fields and serve as feeders to the various branches of the United States military. The websites for these service academies are:

U. S. Coast Guard Academy	www.cga.edu
U.S. Naval Academy at Annapolis	www.nadn.navy.mil
U.S. Merchant Marine Academy	www.usmma.edu
U.S. Military Academy at West Point	www.usma.edu
U.S. Air Force Academy	www.usafa.af.mil

These academies cover the cost of education in exchange for a certain number of years of service in the United States military following the completion of degrees. This affordability factor, along with their reputation for academic quality and success in developing character in young adults, makes these military schools extremely competitive, and therefore it is difficult to gain admission. However, this should not discourage high-achieving, goal-driven individuals from applying.

PROFESSIONAL COLLEGES

These specialty institutions help prepare students for careers in the professions such as business, cosmetology, computer programming, physical therapy, nursing, legal studies, transportation, and more. Professional colleges are usually privately owned and subscribe to a set of standards that meet state and profession standards—thus making them a legitimate choice for job preparation. South College in Knoxville, Tennessee, is such an institution, and it is among a very few that hold regional accreditation. Most professional colleges do not go to this degree to assure their credits will be transferable to other accredited two-year and four-year colleges and universities. However, lack of regional accreditation should not deter a student from applying to an institution.

ONLINE HIGHER EDUCATION

Before we look at private colleges, online education should be mentioned since many public and private institutions have made it available. The hope is that by opening up their offerings to a broader community they can serve more students, as well as benefit from the added enrollment and revenue—without using up any residence hall or classroom space. A recent study by Allen and Seaman for the Sloan Consortium provided a glimpse into the online movement and its growth potential.[4] Here are some of the highlights of their study:

> Over 1.6 million students took at least one online course during Fall 2002.
>
> Over 1/3 of these students took all of their courses online.
>
> Among all U.S. higher education students in Fall 2002, 11 percent took at least one online course.
>
> The number of students taking at least one online course is projected to increase by 19.8 percent the next year.

Those statistics are surprising, aren't they? It goes to show that your collegebound student may be a part of online education.

Flexibility and portability are quite appealing for a society on the move. Assuming they have Internet access, students can stay linked to their college courses, as well as their instructor and classmates, whether they are at home, at the library, or on vacation. Of course, the Internet linkage is not required all the time, as students can work on their reading assignments and papers offline.

Online education affords students the benefit of being able to take courses from home on a part-time or full-time basis. Another benefit is that students only pay for tuition, fees, and books, and therefore save money on room and board charges. Besides those college students solely enrolled in Web-based education, it's increasingly common for students at traditional colleges and universities to add online classes in addition to their standard academic load. This allows them to work ahead on their degree requirements or retake a course during the semester or over summer break.

It's good to know that federal, state, and institutional financial aid programs are usually offered at institutions providing online education. Just be aware that colleges and universities will typically require your student to take at least six semester (or nine quarter) credit hours. If you're interested in inquiring about aid options, just check with a college's financial aid office for details.

As parents, you need to know that there are some in educational circles who object to online education, believing that it is a lower-quality learning experience compared to a traditional pedagogical approach. My position is that both online and traditional educational delivery systems can be effective in our children's learning. I've known of students who have done better with online classes than a traditional education, and vice versa. If we go back to the basics and remember that the main objective is for our students to demonstrate adequate mastery of the course content—any number of delivery systems may be effective in achieving that goal. The previously mentioned Allen and Seaman study confirms that "A majority of academic leaders (57 percent) already believe that the learning outcomes for online education are equal to or superior to those of face-to-face instruction."[5] I think it's important to note that the traditional classroom can be a place where teaching is engaging . . . or dull and irrelevant. A lot depends on the professor. The same is true with online courses. Crummy software and program design can lead to a terrible educational experience; or if it is a solid system, it can be a wonderful way to learn. So a lot rides on course designers *and* professors.

But you may be asking, "So should my child enroll in an

online degree program or not?" My response is—it depends! Specifically, it depends on your child and how she is wired. In order to have a good probability of succeeding, she needs to be disciplined, self-motivated, have good study skills, and have some accountability to assure progress. Some students need and want the traditional approach to college with classrooms, libraries, residence halls, tennis courts, and gymnasiums. They benefit from the live interaction that a campus-based experience affords them.

Certainly, this is the way that we've done college in the Western world for nearly four hundred years—but it doesn't mean this approach is for everyone now that online is a viable option. Some students benefit greatly from online classes and handle them very well. Many of the institutions offering online programs provide access to faculty members and fellow students for class discussions via electronic bulletin boards. They also provide links to the college's library for resources to assist students with research needed for papers, projects, and presentations. Student services are also provided online with connections to people in various departments who can assist them with needs such as transcripts, financial aid, counseling, billing, and career services.

Keep in mind that even if your child is enrolled at a traditional college or university, she can supplement her degree program with online classes. It's always wise to talk with the registrar's office at the "home" institution before registering for online classes to make sure those credits will transfer to that college. If your student is enrolled at a state school, she might want to take some Bible classes through a Christian college's online program. Even if the credits don't transfer because the class is outside the prescribed curriculum, it may be the supplement that helps your student persist in her faith in the midst of antagonism she may be facing in class or the dorms.

All that to say online course work is a legitimate option. It is very attractive because of its portability, pricing, and flexibility for busy students. You may even find yourself wanting to take a class this way!

PRIVATE COLLEGES

As mentioned earlier, this broad category includes 2,456 colleges throughout America enrolling 3.5 million students. There are a number of distinguishable groupings of institutions under the private college heading. For this book I'm using some general categories of Ivy League, Liberal Arts, and Christian. The National Association of Independent Colleges and Universities (NAICU) is a major agency that looks out for the interests of the broad category of private colleges and universities, and they are based out of Washington, D.C. (www.naicu.edu). We'll take a brief look at each of the private college designations.

Ivy League

These prestigious universities are primarily located in New England and other northeastern states and have strong reputations as the academic elite of our country. The names are familiar, and they include Brown, Columbia, Cornell (privately and publicly funded), Dartmouth, Harvard, Pennsylvania, Princeton, and Yale. They feature highly credentialed faculty, well-stocked library collections, and endowments in the billions. Gaining access to these institutions usually costs a great deal of money in tuition, room, board, and fees. In recent years, however, Ivy League institutions have begun making more financial aid available to underprivileged, needy students. Gaining a degree from these places usually ensures that doors will open for their graduates because of their reputation.

Most of the Ivy League universities were founded in the 1600s as institutions to train the clergy—and were therefore very religious in their early years. However, each of them has moved away from those faith moorings and grown increasingly secular in orientation. Campus ministry groups and local church involvement are a must for students attending these universities.

Liberal Arts Institutions

This segment of private colleges and universities has a strong commitment to educating students broadly and deeply, which is what the word *liberal* means in this context. Their curriculum is heavy in subjects that expose students to a broad spectrum of fields of knowledge in the humanities, social sciences, natural sciences, and religion.

These colleges were often founded by church leaders of certain denominations. The Presbyterians, Lutherans, Baptists, and other sectarian groups started their own colleges to educate students broadly, but also to relay the unique doctrinal teachings of their denominations. Today, some of these schools still acknowledge their spiritual heritage, but through the years most have slowly departed from the intent of their founding fathers. Some of these colleges would prefer that no reference be made to their religious heritage, because it runs counter to their current institutional character. However, it is important to note that there are some liberal arts institutions that *have* held to their spiritual moorings, and they are high-lighted in the next section of this chapter.

Liberal arts colleges have long been known for quality, focusing on undergraduate education. In the past twenty years many of these schools have broadened their offerings, adding graduate programs in areas where they have strength and where demand is strong. While much of their education is delivered in traditional time frames during the daytime, a growing number of liberal arts institutions are adding flexible programs for working adults to take classes in the evenings, weekends, or even online.

Most have smaller enrollments, which allow them to focus on people as individuals and provide smaller class sizes than larger colleges and universities. Many of these schools dot the landscape of rural and suburban America and go relatively unnoticed. Their smaller budgets limit the amount of promotional acclaim they can gain compared to schools that have deeper financial pockets; however, you can be assured that most of their resources and energies go toward offering top-quality education for students.

Christian Colleges

Most Christian parents understand these colleges to be focused on Christian precepts. However, many times the public assumes that because those schools are committed to Christ that the degree of intellectual engagement that students experience is limited. They are viewed by some as elevated Sunday schools. That is a misconception. Most of them are academically rigorous and cover a wide span of intellectual and philosophical viewpoints. The difference from their secular counterparts is that those viewpoints are evaluated through the filter of the

Bible. To me, that gives Christian higher education a significant advantage over its secular counterpart. And Christian colleges seek to prepare their graduates not just for making a living but also for a life of service and significance.

Another assumption is that the only career choice of Christian college graduates is ministry. While full-time ministry is a valid career, thousands of graduates of Christian colleges have gone on to work in law, business, medicine, politics, technology, engineering, research, and education—seeing their vocation as a platform to allow them to minister to people who would otherwise not come into contact with a Christian. What a great way to introduce people to Christ, through being what Jesus called salt and light (Matthew 5:13–14).

Christ-centered colleges and universities are often split up into two categories, Christian liberal arts colleges and Bible colleges.

Christian liberal arts colleges offer a liberal arts curriculum that includes an integration of the Christian worldview into classes, as well as Bible courses. The residence life program is also uniquely Christian in orientation, with many activities to help students grow and develop in their relationship with Christ. While not required at most of these schools, Christian ministry or community service programs are offered to encourage students to be outreach-oriented amidst living in our generally self-absorbed society. The majority of Christ-centered liberal arts institutions are members of the Council for Christian Colleges and Universities (CCCU), an association based out of Washington, D.C. (www.cccu.org).

Bible colleges make up the second category. These institutions serve a significant role in the realm of higher education. They primarily serve as educational centers to help students become biblically literate, able to discern the truth, as well as capable servants in ministry as 2 Timothy 2:15 says:

> *Do your best to present yourself to God as one approved, a workman who does not need to be ashamed and who correctly handles the word of truth.*

Thousands of students have studied at and graduated from these institutions, which are scattered throughout the United States. And as their mission statements and outcomes surveys profess, most enter ministry-related careers in churches, missions, and in a multitude of Christian parachurch organizations. Most students enrolling at Bible colleges feel called to the ministry and therefore follow that vocational path throughout their lives. The majority of Bible colleges are members of the Association for Biblical Higher Education (ABHE) headquartered in Orlando, Florida (www.abhe.org). While most are small in numbers, the importance and significance of their graduates should not be underestimated. The fact that the majority of these Bible colleges have people "sold-out" to ministry is powerful because God does great things with their obedience to serve Him and others. With all their hearts, they are going around the corner and around the world to expand the kingdom of God through evangelism, church planting, Bible translation, discipleship, and the list continues. God works through His Holy Spirit to bring about spiritual multiplication, which makes the significance and impact of each Bible college graduate monumental.

5

Criteria for Narrowing the Choices

How do we choose among all these colleges?" asked the mother of a high school senior during a college fair in Jackson, Michigan. As one of the representatives at this event, I quickly shared that the best way to narrow the choices is to define the criteria that they find important. This is advice that I have not only given to families in my professional life through the years but the same advice I personally practiced a week earlier in assisting my oldest son, Andrew, in his college search. Plain and simple—and it works. Of course, each student's criteria will vary to some degree—and may even change as the search continues, but the criteria-based approach to college search is very useful. It is possible to logically walk through the college search process and narrow down the possibilities.

Without determining what is important, the whole search process can be agonizing, and for some people, paralyzing. This chapter provides a comprehensive list of common criteria that can help collegebound students and their parents refine their list of college options. These include:

> Major
> Extracurricular interests
> Reputation and quality
> Distance from home
> Designation
> Cost
> Support system for spiritual walk
> Faculty-to-student ratio
> Personal attention
> Career services
> Personal preferences

MAJOR

One of the first and easiest ways parents and their collegebound student can narrow the list of colleges is through identification of his potential major(s) and career interests. These determinations are largely dependent on his strengths and passions. By the time your teen has completed his freshman or sophomore year of high school, interests should be developing which will be useful in beginning to work toward a career direction. The days of following the career steps of Mom or Dad are increasingly rare. While you still occasionally hear of a member of the next generation acquiring the family business or practice, today's college graduates are mobile and considering a wider variety of options.

Good indicators of your teen's possible college major or career include spiritual gifts inventories, interest inventory assessments, and standardized college testing—in addition to looking at factors as simple as the hobbies and experiences he's enjoyed. There are a couple of resources from Christian ministries that I recommend. Crown Financial Ministries offers a survey through their Career Direct Guidance System, which is designed to help young adults discover their God-given design and talents (www.crown.org). The other is Focus on the Family's *The Call* online assessment tool that helps teens (age 16 and above) discover God's calling in their lives. Taking into account spiritual gifts as well as interests, aptitude, and ability, this resource provides another way to identify vocation and ministry options (www.focusonyourchild.org). The cost of both of these resources is modest compared to the value they hold in pointing your student toward compatible majors and careers. With the results, your student can search for institutions that have good programs in his areas of strength and interest.

The easiest way to find colleges that offer his desired major is via the Internet. There are a number of websites that can perform searches based upon certain criteria, with one of those being major. Recently, my son Andrew and I went through this process on www.christiancollegementor.org. We plugged in his current major of interest, as well as some other search criteria. Within a few seconds we had a list of schools to consider. There are other excellent sites like this including:

www.collegenet.com

www.petersons.com

www.collegeview.com

www.princetonreview.com

www.schoolsintheusa.com

Most students have a lot of different interests, so yours may need to explore a number of majors/careers along the way. So don't be surprised if he occasionally changes his mind.

EXTRACURRICULAR INTERESTS

Besides academics, a big part of the college experience takes place outside of the classroom. Activities such as sports, journalism, student government, music, theatre, Greek life, and many other involvements are all possible search criteria. For example, some friends of our family are seeking colleges that offer equestrian studies as a major . . . or at least provision for their daughters to board the horse they share on campus. For my son Andrew, track and field is an interest he is including in his searches. While for some, extracurricular interest is not that big of a deal, to others it is essential to where they will go to college.

REPUTATION AND QUALITY

The reputation and quality of colleges is somewhat of a subjective concept to define because there are differing views on what makes an institution reputable. To one family, the fact that an institution has enrolled one hundred National Merit Scholars means quality, while another family may view the

U.S. News & World Report rankings as a measure of quality. Some may view quality and reputation by the record of the school's athletic teams, while another family might value institutions because of job placement rates. But one thing is for sure. Whatever you think quality is—you need to be convinced that the colleges you're considering meet the standards that you find acceptable. There are objective measures, which assure that quality is present in higher education institutions. These include factors such as accreditation, licensure, and outcomes data (evidence of espoused intent being fulfilled). I like the definition Bogue and Sanders used in their book, *The Evidence for Quality:* "Quality is conformance to mission specification and goal achievement—within publicly accepted standards of accountability and integrity."[1] I believe that is what you want to be looking for when considering colleges' quality. Are they fulfilling respectable benchmarks? They should have assessment data to share with you if you ask.

Parents often ask about how important accreditation is to where their kids go to college. Institutions that hold regional, national, professional, and program accreditation take quality seriously. It's a seal of approval. It means that they meet certain criteria established by the appropriate agency—which translates into legitimate education and services being offered to students. If you're interested in reading more about accreditation, the Council for Higher Education Accreditation (CHEA) offers a helpful website which describes accreditation in detail (www.chea.org).

Some families do get caught up in the allure of "name-brand" colleges and universities, and are willing or able to pay the high cost of attending those prestigious institutions. A friendly warning: If you're aspiring to send your student to one of these high-profile institutions, be careful to preview their timelines and applicant requirements in advance. Their deadlines may be sooner than you expect.

Distance from Home

It's not surprising that enrollment trends at most colleges reflect a high percentage of students who are from the local area or within their home region. This has been true of all of the colleges and the university where I attended or held employment. While the profile of colleges and universities may tout that they have students from all fifty states and twenty-five countries, the fact is that they may only have a few from some of the more distant states. For example, Moody enrolls about half of its students from the Midwest region, while the Pacific Northwest has less than five percent representation.

If branching out and getting away from home is an objective for your student, there are plenty of college options and plenty of good reasons to do so! However, you all need to be aware that choosing a college across the country may mean fewer visits back home, the possibility that later job or ministry possibilities may be in that region, and if your student meets someone "special," that may also be a determinant of post-college location.

Going to college closer to home can mean lower costs, as well as opportunities for your student to stay connected with family and friends, continued involvement in the local church, and/or keeping a local part-time job.

DESIGNATION

Some families take for granted the institutional type, such as the private or public designations mentioned in chapter 4. The difference between the two is that public institutions operate at the will of states, are for the benefit of the public interest, and are funded through tax money and others friendly to the college. Private institutions are self-supporting without the help of federal or state monies for their basic operational expenses. However, even though private institutions are not allocated state funds, most do allow their students to receive state and federal financial funds (Title IV), which provides support to private institutions' eligible students.

COST

The cost of college is a looming reality for most families and needs to be considered as one criterion used to narrow the list. However, don't automatically rule out colleges because of their cost. Sure, you need to be realistic, and if you haven't saved a lot for college and your family income is modest, an Ivy League institution may be beyond your reach.

When talking about college finances, you need to be aware that there is the "sticker price" and there's the "net price," the amount you actually owe after financial aid. Even if parents have saved for college, they are usually surprised at how much it ends up costing. You'll be interested to know that there are college cost calculators on the Internet to help you determine how much needs to be saved to pay for college. You might think it is a little late to start now, but believe me, every bit helps—and will reduce the amount that you and your student will be faced within payments while in school and in loans afterward. I'm a firm believer that parents need to contribute toward their children's college education—before, during, and in some cases afterward (if loans are used). See chapters 7 and 8 for more information on college costs, the value of an education, and financing this investment.

SUPPORT SYSTEM FOR SPIRITUAL WALK

While not on the majority of college search websites' radar screen, this is one criterion that you'll want to read about in the colleges' brochures and webpages, as well as inquire about in your direct contacts with the admissions personnel at colleges. The Great Commandment is to "Love the Lord your God with all your heart and with all your soul and with all your mind" (Matthew 22:37). You need to think about how and where your student will grow spiritually while in college. It doesn't just happen by default.

Even in a Christian college context, where students are exhorted from the Word of God in the classroom and worship together in chapel, they need to actively and intentionally develop their relationship with Him.

You'll notice as you look at colleges that most have community service opportunities. Around state colleges and universities, the campus ministry organizations offer many opportunities to live out the Christian life. At Christian colleges you'll find offices and personnel that coordinate ministry and service programs throughout the school year and during spring and summer breaks. Regardless of the type of school, don't forget to do some research and visit a few churches in the communities that surround the colleges you visit.

FACULTY-TO-STUDENT RATIO

How important is getting to know professors to your son or daughter? Some students not only want smaller class sizes (ratio of less than 1:20), but want to get together with professors after class, see them at campus events, hang out with them at the student center, and perhaps even go to their homes for meals and relaxation. With lower faculty to student ratios, professors can take on a more relational role, including mentoring and advising.

Other students are not as concerned with the faculty-to-student ratio, but rather are more concerned that the professors are competent in teaching, research, writing, and community service. Other parts of their college experience will meet their relational needs. What they want from the faculty is competence and effective communication of the course content.

PERSONAL ATTENTION

Is your student looking for a college that knows who he is, or is he desirous of staying fairly anonymous? Some colleges and universities go to great lengths to assure that students are known and cared for during their undergraduate experience. Many people automatically assume that small colleges are personal and big universities are impersonal. While it probably tends to work that way, there are exceptions. Some large universities intentionally have smaller affinity groups programmed into their student service areas to allow students to get to know people and to feel like they have something to contribute to that community. And just because a small college *could* yield an environment that is highly personalized, it doesn't guarantee that students will experience that type of intimacy. Some small-college contexts can appear very closed to new students, not making them feel very welcome.

When I first started attending the University of Tennessee in Knoxville, an institution of approximately 25,000 students, my expectations for personal service were not very high. However, I was pleasantly surprised with how interested the various departments, and especially my faculty members, were in caring for my needs as a student. That's definitely something to watch for during your campus visits.

CAREER SERVICES

More and more families are considering the services provided by institutions' career development offices as a part of the criteria. After all, if you get a decent undergraduate education and find it difficult to enter the workforce or get into graduate school—that doesn't say a lot for the institution, does it?

Career development offices typically offer internships or practicums, in conjunction with the academic departments. Essentially, these opportunities provide students with first-hand experiences in their fields of choice. Career specialists at colleges are equipped to help your student make the right kind of connections—making her more marketable, even while she is still enrolled in college. It is common that students who participate in internships or practicums are more employable than those who have not taken advantage of experience-building opportunities.

Career development personnel also assist in job, ministry, or grad school placement before and after graduation. They have connections with potential employers and graduate schools that can be invaluable to your student.

However, resources and expertise will not result in any benefit to your student if he doesn't connect with them—or utilize them early enough. Some schools' departments make special interest sessions available for students to prepare them for what's ahead. Session topics can include resumé writing, interviewing, networking, and etiquette.

As you set up campus visits, ask the admissions department to schedule a time for you to meet the career development personnel and take a tour of their facility, perhaps while your student is sitting in on a class.

PERSONAL PREFERENCES

Just about everyone has them. Some guys may want a single-gender military academy, while some young ladies might prefer a women's college. American Indian students may prefer a college environment on a reservation that is sensitive to Native American customs and culture. There may be an author that you and your student admire who works as a professor at a certain institution. Parents who have home-educated their child may want to make sure the colleges they're considering have a history of enrolling homeschoolers and are welcoming to them. One student may want to experience being in-residence at a college, while another may want to live at home and commute, or even get his degree online from home.

A variety of study-abroad opportunities can be a personal preference. You'll find that many colleges have developed relationships with international institutions around the world— and in many cases those are in conjunction with other U.S.

institutions. The website www.studyabroad.com provides information on hundreds of opportunities for semester or summer programs. Another source is through the Council for
Christian Colleges and Universities, which offers a number of
study abroad programs that bring together students from
the various campuses with a Christ-centered focus (www.
bestsemester.com).

Doing your investigative work on your search criteria will
take an investment of time, but be assured that God will bless
your diligence. There will be ups and downs along the way,
but be patient and persistent. Sorting through the data you
collect will make it more apparent which institutions you
really need to focus on and pursue during the closing months
before the decision date.

FINE-TUNING THE DECISION

After narrowing down your options, you may find that
there are still a number of colleges that fit your criteria. For example, let's say that you have five colleges left on your list
which fit your preliminary criterion of the university having
an in-state designation. Since most states are fairly large in
land mass or population, you could narrow down the colleges
to those closest to where you currently live, or those farthest
away—whichever is most desirable to your child. Another way
to do this is to critically examine the major your student is
planning to enter and determine which institution has the
program best suited for her. Perhaps one of them has more
professors, or a better placement rate of graduates. Of course,
there are other things that may help you determine the best
choice such as scholarships, the overall financial aid package,

and what is discovered during campus visits—all three of which are discussed in the next chapters.

As the decision process winds down, it's important for parents to take a step back with their collegebound student to evaluate all the criteria and see where things stand. Academic rigor, cost of education/scholarships, availability of student activities, distance from home, diversity of the campus community, and a support system for faith—all are important considerations, as we've seen.

Of these factors, the premier one you need to be convinced and deliberate about is the development of your student's faith. As Christian parents, that one is *non*negotiable. Placing your children in an environment where you know he will grow in his relationship with Christ is essential. It's more important than holding a place on the university drama group, more critical than paying a few hundred dollars more per month in the school's payment plan, or more essential than being at a name-brand, top-tier school. Too often, parents assume that a well-known, ranked college or university is the best place, without remembering that the faith of their child is at stake. Whether private or public, don't assume anything. Also be aware that two Christian students going to the same institution does not guarantee the same outcome for each one. Each is prepared differently, experiences different things, makes individual choices —which all affect the outcome.

But during these college years, our kids make lifetime decisions in many areas of their lives—including what they're going to do with God. It's your job to make sure they're placed in a college or university where they'll grow in Him. If there is any ambiguity lingering out there regarding whether your student is ready or if the institution you're jointly leaning toward is the right place—have the courage to reconsider the decision. You either need to help your student fast-track to be ready for college, have him sit out of college for a while, or consider another place.

6

The Campus Visit

A few years ago when my family was back in western Pennsylvania visiting Carolyn's mom, we stopped to visit her alma mater, Geneva College, in Beaver Falls. One of Carolyn's friends was on staff at the time and gave us a tour of the campus—with our four young children in tow. It was a walk down memory lane for Carolyn; for me, a glimpse into her college experiences as she shared the people, places, and memorable events that took place while she was an undergrad on this campus; but for our kids, it was a bit boring. To them, the most memorable thing about the visit was the vast cereal selection in the student dining room! Take your kids on a campus visit when they are between the ages of four to nine and see what they remember!

You're going to be much more successful with campus visits when your children are in their mid- to late-high school years. The interesting thing is that when you step foot on the campus of a college, you're flooded with impressions. Suddenly, your expectations are either confirmed or denied. Up until that point, you've been developing these expectations as a result of information you've been digesting. You've heard things from friends, looked at brochures, scanned websites, and talked to admissions people on the phone. Once on campus, you're experiencing a snapshot of college life and assessing whether this might be the place for your student.

There are two types of college visits, which I term *exploratory* and *determinative*. The exploratory visits represent the initial opportunities to view college campuses and gather information to help ascertain if further consideration will take place. These initial visits normally take place before the senior year of high school and help students ascertain where they will apply. If your student can't visit all the colleges she is considering, check to see if those websites have online tours. There is also a website you might want to look at which includes campus tours of hundreds of colleges. It can be found at www. campustours.com.

The *determinative* visits are ones that involve the schools where your student has applied and are for the purpose of making a final choice. These typically take place in the senior year of high school and many times are tied to special interest weekends, such as "Engineering Day," or for a scholarship competition.

I recommend that you visit the campuses of all your top schools that match your criteria. More and more, parents are accompanying their teens on college visits to consider all there is to see and do. The value of these visits is considerable as evidenced by a 2004 study conducted by the Art & Science Group. Of all the factors that led students to apply to their top schools, 65 percent said that campus visits were most influential.[1] This same study also noted that the average number of colleges visited by prospective students was three.

Since parents are involved in the decision-making process, it makes sense for Mom and/or Dad to be a part of the visits. Students will notice certain things about colleges, and parents will see other things. The drive back home following the visit can be a great time to reflect on what each of you saw and did. After several visits, it is natural to begin comparing and contrasting, which typically results in a narrowing of the options.

Here's a point of clarity for you in preparing for college visits. One of the biggest mistakes parents and their students can make is initiating visits without an agenda. While you may be somewhat of a free spirit and enjoy spontaneity, just be aware that you can miss a lot of important interactions by not being prepared. This college choice is an important decision and needs your full attention because it will have a lifetime of ramifications. It's not like going on a family trip to Disneyland where you just float along doing whatever happens to be around the corner. The college or university you send your student to will shape her for the rest of her life. You want to make sure she ends up at the college that fits her best and will help her grow and develop. So if you take the campus visits seriously, there is a better chance that your student will end up at a school that is a good fit.

With that in mind, before you start scheduling visits, there are some important things that you need to determine. For instance:

- When should you visit?
- Who should come on the campus visit?

• What should you do during a visit?
• Who should you see on a visit?
• How long should you stay?
• What questions should you ask?

In this chapter, we'll consider these questions.

WHEN SHOULD YOU VISIT?

The best campus visits are those that take place on weekdays when the colleges are in full swing. This allows you to get the most realistic picture of academic and student life. Following this type of schedule also lends itself well to connecting with faculty members and coaches, sitting in on campus meetings or chapels, visiting classes, watching a sporting event, and eating in the student dining room. Doing so will give you a good feel for the college and let you see what things are like on a regular day.

You certainly can visit on weekends and during times when classes are not in session, but your exposure will be limited. Weekend and holiday visits are limited in value not only for your family, but also from the perspective of the admissions department. If you're just curious about the look and feel of a campus and want to do a drive-through tour and look around on your own—there's nothing wrong with that. In some cases, you'll find that colleges have regularly scheduled tours on Saturdays, especially if they are game days for the athletic teams. If you do call to schedule a visit on a weekend, just be sensitive to the fact that the college staff and faculty might not be available.

About ten years ago, while I was dean of enrollment management at Bryan College, two families desired such a holiday campus visit on Thanksgiving weekend. However, they didn't call in advance. Instead, they showed up on campus interested in looking around. As you can imagine, things were fairly quiet, as most people had gone home for the extended weekend. These visiting families bumped into a faculty member who was on campus picking up some papers from his office on Thanksgiving Day. When the faculty member found out they had prospective students with them, he assured them that it was no problem to have a member of the admissions staff come over and give them a tour of the campus. I was the only staff member in town that weekend, so I got the call to handle the visit. The difficulty is that I had just sat down with my family for Thanksgiving dinner when the phone rang. I quickly devoured a plate of turkey and fix'ns, excused myself, and headed over to the college, adjusting my attitude along the way. Upon arrival about twenty minutes later, I was focused and gave them a tour, for which they were very appreciative (both families ended up sending their children to the college). However, I must admit that even with the positive outcome of the visit, their *unannounced* arrival stretched the limit of what prospective student families should expect.

If you're in a job that requires being "on call," you know what that feels like. You know it's your job, yet when the call comes it still seems like an imposition on your personal time. From the perspective of the families, it happened to be a very good time to visit because they had time off from work/school and were in the area for the holiday. So if you're thinking about a weekend or holiday visit to a college, call a couple of weeks in advance and see if arrangements can be made to have someone on staff show you around.

You'll be interested to know that many colleges hold special visitation days that focus on certain majors/careers, special activities, and competitions for scholarships. You may also find that colleges will invite you to special events on campus to give you exposure to various areas of interest such as concerts, art exhibits, debates, sporting events, and/or speaker series. So be watching for these specialized opportunities, which can give you broader and deeper insights than what you would get on a normal day on campus.

WHO SHOULD COME ON THE CAMPUS VISIT?

The answer to that question resides largely with your family and on circumstances surrounding the trip. Many families choose to bring everyone in their family. However, bringing pets is generally a no-no. I do recall a couple of instances when families brought their dogs on the college visit . . . one left the dog in the van, and the other carried the dog the entire time (obviously a small breed). Since most colleges don't allow pets on campus, you should probably make other plans for your four-legged friends. Other than that, bringing family and friends who are interested in the visit is best. The first visit (*exploratory*) to a campus is generally enhanced by having multiple members of the family along so what they see and experience can be discussed afterward.

Just be aware that there can be instances where too many people in your party can be a detriment, especially if there are very young children. If you sense trouble brewing, just have a predetermined plan for one of the parents to "peel off" the tour and care for the needs of the younger child. Even with the most entertaining of tour guides, it pales in comparison to other age-specific stimuli.

Some students visit with their youth groups, which is a good way to get a broad overview of colleges. Journeys such as these for college visits or missions trips can be a lot of fun . . . and sometimes the fun part can get in the way of the primary purpose of the trip. If your student is going on a trip to visit colleges, review the real purpose of the trip with her and what she is expected to do and see while she is there. Maybe come up with a checklist of things to look for at each college that she can take with her. If you're interested in learning firsthand about the colleges, trips such as these often need chaperones, so talk to your student and the youth workers about going. Besides helping make sure the teens are doing well, it might also give you a better idea of what options are available at colleges.

Focused visits (*determinative*) at your top two or three colleges are invaluable. I recommend that the visit include the collegebound student and one or both parents. Things are getting very serious at this point, so you'll want to eliminate as many distractions as possible. During these visits, it's not uncommon for applicants to be auditioning for music scholarships, interviewing for academic grants, or trying out for teams and organizations. Too many other family members can add to the stress of it all and affect your student's performance. Make this time extra special by giving your undivided attention and support.

What Should You Do during a Visit?

The campus visit is a time to experience as much of college life as possible. Certain aspects of campus visits will be the same from college to college, such as taking a campus tour, sitting in on classes, meeting with an admissions counselor, and testing out the food in the dining room. However, your criteria (covered in chapter 5) should be a determinant of how you customize the visit. So if your child is interested in majoring in theatre, requesting a meeting with a faculty member in the drama/theatre department would be helpful. If cost is going to be a major consideration in the college decision, it would be beneficial to meet with a financial aid officer to discuss scholarship possibilities. Or perhaps your student has a learning disability, and you want to make sure the college offers adequate services to assist her in being successful. Those personalized requests based upon your criteria will take some extra effort to get scheduled, but I think you will find that most admissions officers will be happy to assist you in seeing and doing the things that will help you get the best possible picture of their college or university.

Be aware that your student may want to venture out on her own during certain parts of the visit, so give her the freedom to do some things with students or staff and faculty members on her own. You don't want to be smothering. Allowing your student some space will help make the visit experience her own and help her determine where she might best fit. The fact is, some parents do dominate during campus visits. They do all the talking, ask all the questions, and appear to be the sole determiner of college choice. In a recent *Washington Post* article, entitled "Parents Casting a Shadow Over College Applicants," writer Jay Mathews describes the extent to which parents are interfering in the campus visit.[2] Among the top irritants: parents answering for the student, filling out forms for them, and asking most of the questions during campus visits. It is inconsiderate for parents to behave this way, and it can embarrass the student and cause her to disengage from active participation. Even if your student is more reserved or lacks confidence in new situations, encourage involvement. To counteract parental tendency to take charge, some colleges do not allow parents to accompany their students on certain parts of the visit. Sometimes students will acquiesce to their parents, and then they don't ask the questions that are on their minds.

It's not uncommon for colleges to interview students during their visits to campus—and do so with the student alone. Admissions counselors want to get to know the students and hear from them about their dreams and goals for college and beyond. So when colleges ask for this exclusive time with your child, know that it's an opportunity for her to share about herself, her experiences, and where she wants to go in the future. And by the way, it is a good sign that certain colleges are desirous of getting to know students. It reveals how much they value developing relationships, and can be a barometer of a very healthy campus climate. It may feel a bit awkward to let your child go during these times, but it's good preparation for the eventual departure.

WHO SHOULD YOU SEE WHILE VISITING?

A college's number-one resource is its people. After all, *people* provide the means for students to enter college, maneuver through its environment, and thrive academically and socially. Because of that, during your visit you will want to meet with as many people as possible. Of course, it's impossible to meet everyone, but there are certain groups of individuals who are great to connect with during the visit. I'll categorize them into groups:

- Faculty
- Students
- Providers of student services

Deservedly, *faculty* members are largely held in high esteem by their students. They are often among the top intellectual minds in their academic specialization. Most hold advanced "terminal" degrees (i.e., doctorates) in their field and are contributing to the body of knowledge through research, writing, and community service, which deepens the understanding society has about their areas of specialty. These faculty members obviously enjoy their field and typically talk about it whenever given the opportunity—and to anyone who will listen. Who better to connect with during a campus visit than professors who can give your student the inside scoop on the latest in their major/profession? You'll find that they love engaging with students who have inquiring minds, are not afraid to ask questions, and are willing to challenge assumptions. These interactions with faculty, even during the prospective student phase, can make a lasting impression and be a major determinant of whether they feel like they would fit at certain colleges.

Tom Fink, a sociology professor and soccer coach at Philadelphia Biblical University, was one of the best I've encountered at connecting with prospective students and their parents. He had a way of making people feel comfortable with the environment at the university.

Another is Dr. Jeff Bruehl, a business professor at Bryan

College. During the time I had the privilege to work with Jeff, he was like a magnet to campus visitors, making them feel welcome. And he expected others on campus to do likewise. Soon after arriving at Bryan to take a position in enrollment, I was amazed when I found out that he gave extra credit to his business students if they hosted campus visitors in their dorm rooms during the big campus visitation days. He not only saw this as a service to visitors, he realized the value of his business students learning what it meant to identify and meet needs. He saw the service mind-set as a part of his curriculum! Sometimes, we as parents and our students can be a bit intimidated with the idea of visiting colleges, but it's faculty members like Tom Fink and Jeff Bruehl that make higher education less threatening.

Students are another group that you and your student will want to connect with during your visit. Most colleges make student interaction a part of the schedule, but in addition to that, make a point to talk with students who are not on the schedule. You know, sort of the "man on the street" approach, getting spontaneous and enlightening responses from those currently enrolled. As you walk around between classes or appointments, engage them with a question or two. Just simply asking the question, "How do you like it here?" can yield some revealing responses. Inquire about academics, extracurricular activities, and spiritual growth opportunities for students. Of course, be aware that you'll need to talk with more than one student to get a wider range of responses. Finding out from just one student that they are extremely happy or disappointed with their experience isn't enough to confirm or reject the institution. Talking with a number of students really helps determine whether the school is fulfilling its mission as described in its website and printed publications. You don't want fluff—you want real testimony and evidence that the colleges or universities are actually doing what they say they're all about.

Student service professionals are another source of information that you'll want to connect with during your visit to colleges. These people are the ones who will have oversight of your child's development, safety, and support—day in and day out. These departments include admissions, financial aid, academic records, student development, bursar/business office, counseling services, career services, athletics, music, food service, and campus post office/student center—just to name some of the major areas. Talking with representatives from these areas will be very helpful in answering questions about the services available to your student. You may not have questions for the people in all of these areas to start out with, but it's helpful to know who they are so that you and your student have a connection for future interaction.

It's common on campus visits to meet not only with admissions personnel but also with a member of the financial aid staff. They can advise you on the details of applying for federal, state, and institutional assistance. Since each family's situation is somewhat different, it's helpful to talk through things so you know what options are available and steps that are forthcoming.

As mentioned earlier, career development is an often-overlooked area when it comes to campus visits. This is a department that demonstrates an institution's commitment to helping future graduates make a smooth transition to their first jobs or graduate schools, as well as serving the ongoing needs of alumni. I recently visited a medium-sized college, and they have one person who does career development in addition to other responsibilities in the student development department. To me, that doesn't show a lot of institutional commitment. You don't want your child to get to the end of her senior year of college and discover that the school has a lousy career services program.

So, as you can see, the campus visit is a chance to meet faculty, students, and student service professionals—all people who can provide information to assist you and your child in making the college choice.

HOW LONG SHOULD YOU STAY?

That's a good question, isn't it? Is it one afternoon, one day, a day and one night, or longer? The answer is—it depends!

One thing is for sure—when it comes to your campus visits, you'll want to allow enough time to adequately see and do all the things important to your son or daughter. I'm not sure why some parents try and squeeze in five colleges in three days—but it happens. This is one of the most important decisions affecting your child's future—so why the hurry?

Well, it usually happens when a dad does the planning, especially if he's the type A, overachiever personality. He's the one who also doesn't stop often enough for restroom breaks while driving on vacations! His approach is to squeeze in as much as possible, in as little time as possible. While this may allow you to cover a lot of ground in a short period of time, the outcome is not always the best. But let me tell you what often happens as a result of this "conquer the mountain" approach. After the first couple of colleges, everything just starts running together in the mind of your student, thus minimizing the uniqueness and memories of each college or university.

Sometimes you don't have the luxury to visit one college per trip. In the case of vacation trips, doing several initial *exploratory* visits to schools is a logical idea. I've seen this fairly frequently with missionaries who visit multiple colleges and universities during home assignment or furlough.

You'll want each visit to stand out. Then, as you consider each one, you'll want to run the information through the grid of your search criteria to ascertain which colleges or universities offer the best fit.

At the *determinative* stage, I recommend that you plan to stay at least one day at each of your child's top colleges or universities, preferably with an overnight so your student can have the opportunity to stay in one of the residence hall rooms with current students. While some colleges and universities may offer parents access to guest rooms on campus, the majority will refer you to local hotels for your lodging. Investing at least a day on campus is a sufficient amount of time to see and do most everything—and not get to the point of your child feeling like they are inconveniencing those students who are hosting her/him.

WHAT QUESTIONS SHOULD WE ASK WHILE VISITING?

The questions you ask will largely be driven by the criteria that you have established before the visits. Some of the common questions include:

• What is the primary role of faculty members? How is their time split between activities such as teaching, research, writing, and community service?

- What is the average faculty tenure (years employed) at your school?
- How would you describe your residence life program?
- What opportunities are available for involvement in student government, work-study programs, and internships?
- What percentage of your faculty holds doctorates/terminal degrees?
- What is your freshman to sophomore retention rate and graduation rate?
- What are your job placement rates?
- What percent go on to graduate school or are accepted into medical school, etc?
- If a public institution, ask about how Christian students interact in their campus environment.
- If a Christian college/university, ask about the kinds of opportunities that are available for Christian ministry or community service.

You'll commonly find statistics or ratios mentioned in admissions literature, websites, and on campus tours. These can be defined as *features* of the colleges. But what do the *features* mean to you as a family visiting a college or university? They might sound impressive and mean something to somebody. But you may need to probe a little bit and ask the "so what" question. In other words, when people tout statistics, ask them what are the benefits of each feature.

You may be asking yourself, "Okay, what should we do following the visit? Is there some sort of protocol for follow-up that is necessary?" If you found your admission officer to have been especially helpful in handling your visit, you or your student might want to send him or her a thank-you note or e-mail. Otherwise, your most important follow-up is to sort through everything you learned on each visit and run it though the criteria grid you developed earlier. There may be multiple colleges that meet most of your criteria, so if your student is a senior, she should go ahead and apply to each of her top schools so she can be considered for the deadlines related to admission, scholarships, and financial aid.

As I reflect back on my first college visit trip while a high school junior in the late 1970s, I remember the excitement as well as the anxiety that was generated as a result. This tour of colleges took place in the southeast region of the United States with a couple dozen other high school kids from churches in my area of Ohio, Indiana, and Michigan. My parents didn't come along on this trip. It was a whirlwind experience—riding on a coach bus from college to college trying to capture the essence of each campus and attempting to determine if any of them might be an option. We experienced all kinds of dorm situations, college meals, and campus activities. Of course, as much as I learned about colleges, the trip was a taste of what college would be like. It was a lot of fun! In fact, the trip helped me determine for sure that I needed to go to college. It turned out that I didn't enroll at any of the schools we visited, but the experience did help me know more of what was available and helped me ascertain things I liked and disliked.

A practical note about taking time off from school to go on campus visits. High schools commonly require a letter from the college stating your child was on a campus visit. The schools use this information in tracking attendance. If your child is enrolled at a traditional school, check with the guidance office for details.

Your campus visit experiences will likely be one of the "clinchers" in helping you and your student make your final choice of a college. Take your time planning the visits, allow adequate time on each campus, and fill that time with valuable interaction with faculty, students, and support staff. You won't regret the time and money invested in this journey.

The Admissions Process

When you and your student get to the point of applying, the college selection process becomes more real, doesn't it? Applying for admission to colleges and universities is an exciting step in the process. It signals that the options have been narrowed down and progress toward the final decision is being made. However, completing applications along with the other requirements such as writing essays and requesting transcripts and references can be time-consuming—especially if your student is applying to a number of colleges (which is a good idea).

You'll be glad to know that applying for admission to colleges has been made much easier in recent years, thanks to the Internet. Most institutions have applications that can be filled out and submitted online. References and essays can also be sent via the Web. A nice feature of many of these online application systems is that they allow students to work for a while, save their work, and come back to it later to

bring it to completion. Also, most of these online application software programs catch any blank fields and don't allow your student to progress until those open fields are filled
out properly. With all this in mind, you should know that
submitting the admissions paperwork in hard copy through
mail delivery could slow the admissions process considerably.
Also, any missing forms such as references, transcripts, test
scores can delay processing, and depending on deadlines, result in rejections from those institutions.

It's interesting that the usage of online applications has advanced so quickly. Some institutions, like the University of
Dayton in Ohio, require all students to submit their applications electronically. In other words, they do not accept paper
applications any longer! Other institutions like the University
of Michigan accept both types of applications, though 60 percent of applications in 2003 were filed electronically.[1] Some of
us parents have a hard time with the idea of going paperless,
but rest assured, it generally works well, and students enjoy
the benefits of using technology in this way. And you can
count on colleges to keep your student's information secure
and not share it with other institutions, organizations, or companies. But if your student really wants to apply the traditional
way with paper and pen, many colleges still accept applications in that form. However, that may not last for too many
more years.

There are coalitions of colleges that cooperate with electronic applications and share application data with each other,
if students are interested in multiple schools within the co-
operating group. Examples of these include www.commonapp.
org and www.xap.com. These are referred to as shared or common applications. The benefit of this for students is that they

fill out one application and can choose to send it to multiple colleges, assuming they're a part of the cooperative network. Just be aware that even though your student fills out one application for multiple institutions, a separate application fee is due at each one. Application fees for colleges are usually around $25–$50 and are nonrefundable.

Through the years, I've found that a high percentage of prospective students delay completing their applications because of the essays that most colleges require. Writing an essay can be enjoyable, but for some students it's dreaded. Let your student know that the questions typically aren't all that hard to answer; it's just that the process is time-consuming. A lot of students have a hard time getting started because they think the first draft has to be in finished form. Encourage your student to start out by sketching an outline of general points of response to the questions on their computer's word processing program. Then gradually he can add or delete details to his outline points. Going about this logically and gradually takes some of the pain out of the process—especially if he starts in advance and allows the essays to develop over time. If he waits until the night before the application deadline to start writing, it will be *a night to remember* and likely won't represent him as well as if he had worked on it in advance. As an admissions officer for sixteen years, it was obvious when evaluating application files which students were careful and thorough and which were careless filling out their forms and writing essays. At some schools, a hastily prepared application can diminish chances for admission. So encourage your student to start on it a few weeks before it needs to be sent and encourage him to be careful to do a good job with the presentation of admission materials.

While the majority of collegebound students apply in advance of deadlines, there are always some who wait until the last minute to complete the process.

I still remember our admissions staff at Bryan College scrambling around the day before new students were to report for orientation—helping evaluate the application files of a couple of last-minute procrastinators attempting to gain acceptance to the school. This is not something to aspire to—because for one, many colleges have application deadlines and will not consider late applicants. Many colleges will be at capacity by midsummer. Secondly, waiting until the last minute doesn't allow students to carefully consider the decision. Many factors go into the college decision, and to make it in a compressed manner generally doesn't allow for a full consideration of criteria. Third, the resulting effect is that retention rate for last-minute students is always lower than students who planned in advance. It's like a person marrying someone he just met on a blind date. There's a higher probability of a bad decision, and departing before graduation is not good for the student or for the institution. So it's often not good stewardship of time or money to enroll at the last minute.

Therefore, if for some reason your student is getting started late, I'd encourage him to wait a semester or a year before enrolling in college. He will be better off in the long run since it's a decision that ought to be well thought out.

I do recommend that students apply to more than one college to assure that they have options if they are not accepted to their first-choice college.

Submitting the Paperwork

It's important that teens submit their admission materials in advance of the published deadlines. If this information was completed using paper forms, be sure to have them mailed to *arrive* in advance of the deadlines. This includes the reference forms that important individuals (teachers, guidance counselor, youth minister, employer) will fill out for them. In fact, with this group, it's a good idea to provide postage-paid, addressed envelopes so that it's easier for them to get them mailed in time. If you're among the growing number of families who will take advantage of an online admission process, just about everything can be sent electronically. This is a fast and efficient way to deliver materials to the colleges and universities. It is also beneficial to the institutions because the majority of the information you send in will flow directly into their databases—alleviating the need for someone on staff to manually re-enter all the data.

Most colleges and universities will update your student along the way as the various items in his admission file arrive in their offices. If he has submitted items and does not receive an e-mail or letter from the colleges confirming receipt of the forms within a couple of weeks of applying, it is appropriate for him to call the admissions office to ask if they received his forms. In this case, no news is *not* good news. He needs to make sure everything that is needed is received, including the application, application fee, essays, references, high school/college transcripts, and ACT or SAT test scores—especially if there is a deadline for these materials.

In increasing numbers, high school students are acquiring college credits through several means before actually enrolling at a university. If certain scores are achieved on the College Board tests, credits—or at least class exemptions—are awarded at many colleges (www.collegeboard.com). Advanced Placement (AP) classes are offered at many high schools as upper-level options in their curriculum. After taking one of these classes, the AP test can be taken, which can result in college credit. Another possibility is the College-Level Examination Program (CLEP), which offers tests in a number of subject areas. These too are recognized by some colleges as credit. There is a charge per test taken, but it's minimal compared to what it can save you later in college tuition charges. The third option is dual-enrollment classes in which high schools partner with colleges to offer classes that meet high school graduation requirements, as well as earn college credits. There is a tuition charge for these classes since they are partnering with a college, but the cost is usually very reasonable. So keep these options in mind and remember to submit transcripts or score reports to colleges as a part of the application process.

AWAITING ADMISSION DECISIONS

Yes, it's time for the drum roll! Once all of your admission forms are submitted, the admissions offices of the institutions will check over all the materials that you've submitted to make sure they are complete, and then they make sure all the information is correct in their databases.

In the world of college and university admissions there are two primary models of admission processes—rolling admissions and selective admissions. *Rolling admission* is the one that most colleges use. Basically, rolling admission means that as applicants complete their admission files, the admissions committee will review those files for acceptance or denial. Under this model, applicants find out soon after applying if they have been accepted to the school or not. Each institution is a little different in the timing of their letters, so be patient. However, if you haven't heard anything within a month, it would be good for your student to contact them about the status of the admission file.

The other model for the admission process is called *selective admission.* This means the institutions are more selective in the applicants they consider and make admittance decisions usually at two points of the year. Essentially they wait until a whole group of applications have been received before making decisions. For many selective colleges and universities, the first acceptance period is December 1 and notifications (acceptance, denial, or decisions to wait) are mailed out by the end of January. A second acceptance period is March 1 and is intended for those applicants who were held over from the December acceptance period, as well as any new applicants who have sent in their materials since then. By the end of March, notifications are sent out for this group of prospective students.

The more prestigious institutions tend to be the ones who offer selective admission. Their applicant pools (number of students applying) are usually full to overflowing, so they can afford to be choosey. But even less-prestigious institutions can still have selective admission, because they reach capacity quickly and have reached the limit on their campus facilities and services.

RECEIVING "THE ENVELOPES"

It is nerve-racking waiting to hear from the colleges about admittance. Of course, students can't enroll at all the colleges that they've applied to—but there's something nice about them being accepted, even at schools they don't end up attending. It's nice to know your kids are acceptable. But if your student isn't accepted, please respond with restraint.

Some colleges (primarily selective ones) have a three-day waiting period after the notification letters go out to allow "hot" parents to cool down a bit before they can call the admissions office and discuss the decisions with them (chew them out).[2] You might think that Christian parents are above this kind of behavior, but trust me, some don't stop with the admissions officer—they go to the alumni director (if they are alumni of the school), the provost, and the president with their protest. At that point there isn't a lot that can be done about the decision. If you really want your child to get into that particular school someday, make the conversation more positive by asking what he can do to improve his profile for the next acceptance period. If that school is not a future possibility, refocus your energies into colleges and universities that have accepted your student.

CONFIRMING INTENT

After receiving acceptance letters from a school, your teen will be asked to confirm his plan by sending an enrollment deposit to the college he intends to attend. Most colleges charge around $100–$250 for these deposits, and those funds typically apply toward some part of the upcoming year's bill.

The national confirmation date is May 1, which is the time colleges will expect your student to notify them of his intent to enroll or not (by sending in their enrollment deposits). Allowing families until May 1 gives them time to consider the offers of admission and the financial aid packages of various institutions. This deadline signals the convergence of the admissions and the financial aid processes in the late spring.

You may be asking, "Can I send a deposit to more than one institution?" My answer is a hesitant yes. There aren't a lot of good reasons for doing this, and the practice is looked down upon by the admissions and financial aid offices, but some parents do this to hold their student's space and financial aid at multiple institutions—to accommodate some unusual reason. However, be aware that some colleges are starting to use the practice of revoking offers of admission if they discover your child has "double deposited." Selective schools such as Amherst College are swapping names of accepted students with other institutions of early-decision applicants to seek out those who have double deposited—removing them from their lists.[3] Other institutions are increasing their deposit amount to discourage this practice. The issue for institutions is, with double depositing they lose their ability to manage the size and quality of their incoming enrollments. The bottom line is that they don't want to be left short when the semester starts.

Keep in mind that most institutions will not refund enrollment deposits after the May 1 deadline—so you'll lose that amount of money if you cancel.

If your student is accepted and he's *not* going to enroll at a certain college, *not* sending a deposit may seem to you as notice enough of his plans to go to another school. But realize that a relationship has developed over time between your student and the college admissions counselors, so it is a cordial gesture if you or your student can e-mail the admissions office and inform them of your child's decision. Not doing so is a bit like when people in high school who were dating would suddenly break up without talking about it. Even though it can be awkward to discuss the breakup and reasons behind it, lack of communication doesn't contribute to understanding between the parties involved. Most institutions truly want what's best for the student's future—so they will understand. It helps bring closure to the relationship and gives you a chance to say thanks for their help along the way.

However, before sending in the deposit, you'll want to consider the cost and the financial aid package before a final decision is made. Chapters 8 and 9 cover the crucial parts of this process.

The Cost
of College

"It costs *what?*" Dad asks. Sticker shock is what most parents experience when they get ready to send their first child to college. Even with the frequent news reports of how fast college costs have risen in the past fifteen years, it doesn't become real until the "they" becomes "us," and we now have a student ready for college. Somehow we're under this illusion that tuition, room, and board charges stand still in time—since we were in college. Have you experienced that yet? If not, hang on—you're about to undergo a wild ride!

HISTORY OF COLLEGE COSTS

Listed on the next page are the average costs of education (tuition, room, and board) over the past few decades by institutional type.[1]

	Public Colleges & Universities (in-State Rate)	Private Colleges
1964–65	$950	$1,907
1969–70	$1,203	$2,530
1974–75	$1,563	$3,403
1979–80	$2,165	$4,912
1984–85	$3,408	$8,202
1989–90	$4,504	$12,018
1994–95	$5,965	$16,207
1999–00	$7,310	$20,186
2002–03	$8,556	$23,503

Keep in mind that these costs are averages, so in each category there are institutions that cost less or more than these numbers (also that the prices go up incrementally on an annual basis). This chart is instructive because it shows the impact of state taxpayer support of public colleges and how it leads to lower costs for in-state students going to those institutions. Out-of-state students can still enroll at public institutions, but it just costs more to attend (similar in cost to a private college). Private colleges and universities, as independent institutions not owned by the states, do not benefit from that same funding allocation as public institutions. Therefore, private colleges do not charge differently based upon students states of residence (it is the same rate for in-state and out-of-state students). To help meet their budgets, these independent schools do a lot of fundraising to help subsidize the ongoing costs of the college. Their fundraising and other efforts to find support to pay for new programs, faculty, and facilities help keep the students' costs at private colleges a little lower.

A Triangulation Effect

You need to know there are three things that have been happening in regard to cost, which is creating challenges for many families. These factors include increasing costs, financial aid staying fairly level, and parents not saving enough.

Just like homes and automobiles, the college education costs have seen steady increases. These are due in part to inflation and increased expenses. It costs money to retain faculty and keep facilities up-to-date. In the midst of these price increases, colleges have been doing more in the form of discounting tuition through institutional financial aid to help needy students afford the education.

The second factor is that federal and state funding of higher education is not keeping pace with expenses, with the result being a widening gap for institutions and those they serve. Many states are not able to fully fund the allocations that have been promised to public colleges and universities because there are so many demands on their state budgets (like K–12 education, health care, and transportation). So instead of colleges getting funded at 100 percent of what they need, the allocation may be less than that level depending on how the overall state budget is doing. Obviously when this happens, it places public institutions in a pinch to find other ways to raise the money to make up the difference. Tight budgets not only at the state level, but also at the federal level, have also kept financial aid to students (Title IV) fairly flat. The resulting impact affects college students at both public and private institutions.

The third factor in this college cost challenge is that many parents have not been disciplined in saving for college. Many things hinder us as parents in saving for college; however, it needs to be more of a priority and an established part of our budgets. Just as we find a way to pay for food, housing, insurance, retirement, and vacations, we also need to have college savings as a line item! The time to start saving, even if it is a little bit late to start, is *now.*

THE GREAT VALUE

These three factors create a triangulation effect that presents a challenge to those who are preparing to send a child to college. However, parents don't need to let the challenges paralyze their ability to help make a college education a reality. The value of college is well documented, so it's worth the effort for us as parents to see our children in colleges that are a good fit.

Speaking of value, the College Board released its report called "Education Pays 2004," which notes the benefits of higher education for individuals and society in general.[2] The benefits to individuals:

- There is a correlation between higher levels of education and higher earnings for all racial/ethnic groups and for both men and women.
- The income gap between high school graduates has increased significantly over time. The earnings benefit to the average college graduate is high enough for graduates to recoup in a relatively short period of time both the cost of full tuition and earnings forgone during the college years.
- Any college experience produces measurable benefit when compared with none, but the benefits of completing a bachelor's degree or higher are significantly greater.

The societal benefits:

- Higher levels of education also correspond to lower levels of unemployment and poverty, so in addition to contributing more to tax revenues than others do, adults with higher levels of education are less likely to depend on societal safety-net programs, generating decreased demand on public budgets.
- College graduates have lower smoking rates, more positive perceptions of personal health, and lower incarceration rates than individuals who have not graduated from college.
- Higher levels of education are correlated with higher levels of civic participation, including volunteer work, voting, and blood donation.

SOURCE: *Education Pays 2004*. Copyright © 2004 by the College Board. Reproduced with permission. All rights reserved. www.collegeboard.com

These benefits help validate the positive role higher education plays in America and around the world. They also show that the investment of our hard-earned money pays dividends throughout our children's lives.

9

Financing the Educational Investment

We can't afford to send our daughter to your college after all," the mother of an accepted incoming student explained to me over the phone one Friday afternoon in May. My mouth must have dropped to the floor, because there were no distinguishable words coming out of it. I couldn't believe it. As I shared the news with others in the admissions and financial aid offices, we were all so disappointed. We felt that way because one of our best prospects for the entering class was about to cancel her plans to enroll—over money. The words of this mother shocked us—particularly because everything up until that point led us to believe that her daughter would be enrolling. The daughter was devastated by this news as well.

As staff members, we repeated the obvious question, "How could this mother not send her daughter after we had awarded her one of the top academic grants given to incoming freshmen, the presidential scholarship?"

This impending decision just didn't feel right, so we made a call back to the mother and told her the scholarship would be held for them over the weekend, if they would reconsider and pray about this some more. Early the next week, I received a phone call from the mother, and she shared that they had found a way to come up with the remaining cost of their daughter's education after financial aid. It turned out that she and her husband decided that she should go back to work since they would be empty nesters when their daughter went to college. They came to realize that this was God's way of providing what they needed and that it was *their* responsibility to step up and make this happen for their daughter.

This story is not unique. Through the years, I've seen God work in amazing ways to help Christian families find a way to enroll their children in their top-choice schools. And it's usually families asking in faith and stretching the borders of what they think is possible. I've witnessed a family decide to sell their twenty-four-foot recreational boat to finance a couple years of college for their son. On another occasion, I was deeply moved at the level of sacrifice as a family in Athens, Georgia, maxed out the equity in their home for a second mortgage to send both of their sons to college at the same time. I've seen cases where students work diligently in the summers and during school breaks to help meet the cost of their education. I've seen churches and friends of the family come forward and contribute funds to help underprivileged youth enroll in college. I recall a number of instances when grandparents stepped in to help meet the cost of education in order for their grand-children to enroll at their first-choice college. And I've seen families be so convinced that a certain college is the right one for their child, that as a last resort they chose to take out some extra loan dollars to pick up the last portion of the cost. Each family situation is different, but remember that God is Jehovah Jirah (the great provider). Be optimistic about the possibilities because of how He can work.

Unfortunately, there are also families that see the sticker price of their top-choice schools and give up before even try-ing. On one hand they don't want to get their children's hopes up—then dash them later because they don't receive enough in financial aid, or they don't have adequate money in savings to cover the cost. It *does* boil down to a family decision, but some parents short-circuit the process by making a decision before seeing what God can do.

In a research study conducted by the Investment Company Institute in 2003, they found that two-thirds of parents were saving for their children's higher education costs.[1] Of the group that had been active, the median amount saved was $10,000 (the mean being $23,600), with the intention of eventually accumulating $35,000 (median)/$92,700 (mean) by the time their oldest or only child is ready to go to college. The study showed that parents had been saving for college an average of 7.4 years. With those figures in mind, if a family has three children, those dollar amounts would need to be split in as many ways.

Seeing from chapter 8 that the 2002–2003 average public college/university cost is $8,556 per year, and the average pri-vate cost is $23,503—most Americans have a lot more saving to do if they're going to pay for multiple years of schooling.

Outside of financial aid, options for meeting college costs besides parent and student savings include monthly cash flow allocations and payment plans.

One of the major intents of this chapter is to share the basics of financial aid so you know more about the programs and how to go about applying for assistance. Before proceeding, though, I'd like to share something—parent to parent. As parents, our role is to assist our children in financing the school bill. However, don't leave your student out of the loop when it comes to the financial side of college. It's an important part of his growth and development to understand the cost of college, how finances work, the value of hard work, and how God supplies. So recognize this as part of the college experience, not as a nuisance. It's actually a part of *his* higher education.

Regardless of where your collegebound teen goes to college, your family is responsible to come up with the resources to pay for college. Does it surprise you that I'd even have to mention that? Perhaps it does, or perhaps it does not. I bring it up because in my experience, some parents seem to think that it is the institution's responsibility or the role of the government to come up with the money to pay their child's school bill. *It is not.* But don't get me wrong—the colleges and government agencies are possible sources of assistance, but you need to accept responsibility for finding a financial plan that works for your family. In some cases that means making hard choices in order to come up with the funds needed to pay for college. For some, that may mean *putting off* vacations, the purchase of a new car or motorcycle, or buying a new house. For others it means going out to dinner less and saving more. For some it means taking on a part-time job—or scouring libraries and the Internet for corporate and civic scholarships.

All this may sound a bit too much like sacrifice. But be re-minded that in Philippians 4:11–13, Paul shares that:

> *I am not saying this because I am in need, for I have learned to be content whatever the circumstances. I know what it is to be in need, and I know what it is to have plenty. I have learned the secret of being content in any and every situation, whether well fed or hungry, whether living in plenty or in want. I can do everything through him who gives me strength.*

We must ask ourselves as parents: "Is there really any better use of our resources than investing in our children?"

Financing the education is a matter of prayer for Christian parents. God works in miraculous ways in certain instances, and at other times He enables ordinary means to provide the way to pay for college. Philippians 4:19 says, "And my God will meet all your needs according to his glorious riches in Christ Jesus." Knowing this, my encouragement to you as parents is to go into the process with the intent to find a way to make your student's college choice a reality. Do all you can to pull together resources from as many sources as possible, not neglecting your own share of contributions. Remember what David said in Psalm 50:10, "For every animal of the forest is mine, and the cattle on a thousand hills." All the resources of the world ultimately belong to God, so why not ask for His provision?

And however God provides, be sure to give Him the praise. Our heart attitude needs to reflect the words of the apostle Paul in the book of Colossians:

> *And whatever you do, whether in word or deed, do all in the*

name of the Lord Jesus, giving thanks to God the Father
through him. (3:17)

This section is organized to show the usual financial aid programs and how to apply for each type. These major categories include institutional aid, government aid, and outside scholarships. I'd encourage you to access the recommended college and financial aid websites for the most up-to-date information because these programs and their criteria do change occasionally.

Institutional Grants and Scholarships

The money that colleges and universities provide to students who meet certain criteria is referred to as institutional financial aid. And you'll be glad to know that it is money that does not have to be paid back. Because each institution is unique, these grants and scholarships vary, as well as their deadlines, from college to college.

Merit aid is a category of financial aid that most institutions offer. It represents money that can be obtained through students' ability or talent levels, as well as "who they are," such as their parents being alumni of the college, being in a certain denomination, or living in a certain county. The major types of merit aid include academic, entitlements, athletic, music, and leadership.

The academic grants (sometimes called scholarships) typically require a certain grade point average (GPA), along with a corresponding SAT/ACT score. They range anywhere from a few hundred dollars to thousands of dollars. You might even find that certain institutions offer a limited number of full-tuition scholarships for their top prospects (but don't expect that at most schools). Most institutions have different grant levels based on these academic averages and scores. At certain places, these academic grants are automatically awarded without extra paperwork, while at other colleges students must compete against others for the dollars. If competitive, these grants are typically determined through special essays and interviews with faculty members in the students' area of study.

Another type of institutional aid that schools make available is sometimes referred to as entitlements. These grants are given because of who you are related to, where you live, and things you've done. For example, at Bryan College, they offer such a program and call it the Heritage Grant, which gives a $1,000 renewable scholarship to students if they meet one of several criteria. These criteria are:

Resident of the county (or surrounding counties) where the college is located

A parent or grandparent is an alumnus of the college

Spouse or parents are in full-time ministry

A parent or grandparent is an active member in the Christian Medical and Dental Society

You'll want to find out about these types of entitlement grants at the colleges you're considering. In some institutions they allow "stacking" of these grants so that they accumulate toward the overall financial award. Another form of entitlement can be obtained through one of the matching grant programs whereby your college partners with your church or designated civic organization, which commits a certain amount of money for your student's education. Then in return, the college matches that commitment up to a certain dollar amount.

Other entitlements are available through a handful of colleges that offer tuition-paid education. Yes, you read it correctly! There is no charge for tuition. "It's too good to be true," you respond! It is good, and it is true. Among these institutions are Moody Bible Institute, College of the Ozarks, and Berea College. Just be aware that there are some stipulations with these types of institutions. At Berea and College of the Ozarks, they have a mandatory work programs for all students —essentially in exchange for the free tuition. Their philosophy is deeply rooted in servanthood as a basis for adequately training and educating students to be contributing members of society. At Moody, there is not a work program or a requirement to pay back tuition. It is free for undergraduates because of the school's desire to see the education be affordable to make it more likely for them to enter ministry roles immediately after graduation, rather than having to delay because of student loan indebtedness. Obviously, these institutions either have large endowments or significant annual giving campaigns, which provide the means of supporting thousands of tuition-paid students. As you can well imagine, these colleges have an abundance of applicants, so if your student is interested, he will need to check out the requirements and be careful to meet their admissions and financial aid timelines.

Athletic grants are typically available to students who meet or exceed minimal academic levels, as well as "make the team," as determined by the coaching staff of colleges or universities. While we often hear about student-athletes who get a full ride, it is rarely the case for most student-athletes. Most are receiving *some* athletic aid based on their abilities, but not *all* the cost of college. In fact, in the NCAA Division III, institutions *cannot* award athletic scholarship money. Schools in this division are competitive in their athletic programs, but they enroll students without athletic scholarships.

If your student is a high achiever in sports, you'll want to check out colleges' teams, coaches, conference, competition, and level of support they give to their overall programs, as well as aid to students. If your child is fortunate enough to get a full ride, the athletic departments cover all the expense of college minus any money for which the student may be eligible because of other forms of financial aid (entitlements, federal, and state aid). Even if your student just gets a portion of his college costs covered by institutional athletic money, be encouraged. This demonstrates that your student has great ability, and the award can be a big help in covering a part of the school bill.

Music grants are another means of institutional aid. These monies are usually reserved for top achieving musicians with promise for musical careers in performance or education. Obtaining music grants almost always requires a music audition on campus with professors in the music department. Usually your student prepares a couple of pieces of music to play or sing—and then performs in front of a panel of professors. Additionally, they may ask her a number of questions about her background, whom she has studied under, and what her aspirations are for the future. Just keep in mind that most colleges are going to award their money to students who are going to major in music. If your student is interested in music as a hobby, he may be able to be involved in college musical groups, as well as take music lessons, but most likely will not receive music department grants.

Performance-based aid will require that your child be actively involved in those activities. "No play, no pay" is a way to
look at it. Institutions may pull the grants if students discon-
tinue their participation, and the school bill will reflect the
difference. But rest assured that colleges will not pull the car-
pet out from under your student without cause. Up front, institutions will make available the conditions for maintaining
good status and retaining awards received.

A good thing to know as you consider all the various institutional grants is renewability. In other words, are the grants
available for the first year only (incentive to get your child to
enroll), or are they renewable (commitment to help him persist through graduation)? Obviously, the renewable grants are
the best because they help add certainty to what the financial
aid package looks like, not just for the first year, but also in future years. Even if grants are renewable, there may be continu-
ance standards. For example, an academic grant may require a
certain college cumulative GPA to keep receiving the assistance. Just research the information that college financial aid
offices provide and these types of issues will be answered. If
you have questions, by all means e-mail or call the financial
aid or admissions offices for clarification.

NEED-BASED FINANCIAL AID

You'll be pleased to know that higher education institutions want to help you determine if you have financial need so
they know whether you'll be eligible for federal and state assistance. You may have heard that if your family makes too much
money, or has too many assets, you might not be eligible to receive need-based financial aid. *But how do you know for sure?*

The answer can be found through filling out some forms provided by the colleges called the Free Application for Federal Student Aid, whose abbreviated name is FAFSA (www.fafsa. ed.gov). These applications give colleges and universities the information needed for determining eligibility for grants, loans and college work-study. Essentially, you input numbers from your 1040 tax forms to determine eligibility. If you're just curious about what you might be eligible to receive, there are a number of websites that give estimates based upon the numbers you enter. These include the following:

www.finaid.org
www.princetonreview.com/college/finance/efc/

Keep in mind that if you use these websites, you'll only get estimates. Completing the real FAFSA is the only way to know for sure. You certainly don't want to miss out on federal and state financial aid possibilities, so I encourage you to file the FAFSA at least the first year. If you apply and aren't eligible for grants (free money), you will have the paperwork submitted to be considered for the work program and/or loan programs.

You may come across some colleges who also have secondary means of assessing financial need. There is such as a program called PROFILE, which is a product of the College Board (https://profileonline.collegeboard.com). This product considers some of the same factors as the FAFSA, but also looks at more detailed factors such as whether your family owns a home (equity). Be aware that there is currently a cost of $5 (plus $17 for each school to which you submit your information). If a variant need-assessment tool like the PROFILE is used, the individual colleges will make you aware of that fact.

In thinking about the governmental financial aid programs, you need to know that they are based upon laws that were established by Congress and are usually referred to as Title IV financial aid programs. From time to time, these programs change, dollar amounts are modified, or conditions for obtaining aid change with legislation. If that happens while your student is enrolled, the changes usually take place in the next annual awarding period. Let's take a look at the longstanding forms of federal financial aid that are in effect at the time of the writing of this book.

Federal Pell Grants

Pell Grants are free money made available to students whose families meet required income and asset levels as determined by the FAFSA. Without exception, this money goes to the neediest of students in our country. And that's the nature and purpose of these monies—to help those who can't afford to go to college otherwise. Some parents don't understand that fact and expect to get a Pell Grant for their child, even though their family income is above the national average. That's not whom these grants are intended to serve. Recipients of Pell Grants are usually at income levels that qualify them to be considered for state grants as well (states look at the FAFSA data too). However, be aware that while the Pell Grants are nationwide, the state grants are unique to each state. Some of the specifications and dollar amounts vary according to what each state legislature puts into place in its budget. Some states give large amounts to needy students, while others provide more modest assistance.

Federal Supplemental Educational Opportunity Grant

This form of aid is allocated by the federal government to be used by individual institutions. It is also intended for the neediest of students. Those eligible can expect to receive between $100–$4,000 per year depending on when you apply, your need, the funding level of the school you're considering, and the policies of the financial aid office of each institution. However, there's no guarantee each eligible student will receive funds. The amounts and awards are determined by each school.

Federal Work Study

As the name suggests, this federal aid program provides funding for students to work on campus to help pay a portion of the school bill. Like other aid programs, Federal Work Study (FWS) is administered by the financial aid office. Again, this program is designed for the neediest of students to help them finance their education. Most of the jobs pay the federal minimum wage, and, of course, are positions around the college campus or community. Essentially, the federal government pays a portion of the wage and the college pays the rest. If your child is eligible for FWS, the financial aid award letter from each college he is considering will include this dollar amount. Based upon the amount of money that each institution has available, the dollar amounts of FWS can vary. Just because FWS is awarded doesn't mean that a job on campus will be available. At times these jobs fill up—especially if your student waits until the last minute before applying for the positions that are available. Another thing to keep in mind is that the FWS amount applies only if the student actually works the hours. Essentially, the money is not payable unless he fulfills his end of the arrangement. It is assumed that the student will use the paychecks from FWS to help pay his educational expenses, rather than for pizza delivery!

Federal Student Loans

There are a number of student loans available for families. One of the most desirable is the Subsidized Stafford Loan and serves students with financial need. This program allows students to borrow a certain amount of money toward their college expenses, and while they are enrolled, the federal government pays the interest on the loan. Currently, dependent undergraduate students can borrow $2,625 their freshman year, $3,500 their sophomore year, and $5,500 for each remaining year. Once the student completes his studies, leaves school, or drops to less than half-time enrollment—he starts making payments six months later and at that point starts paying the principal and interest. Families with lower incomes and assets are the usual beneficiaries of this type of loan.

Also in the Stafford family of student loans, is the Unsubsidized Stafford Loan program (same dollar amount limit as the Subsidized Stafford). This loan is not based on need, and the interest *does* accrue during the college enrollment period. When students finish their studies, leave college, or drop to less than half-time enrollment, they are expected to start making payments, which will include the interest that has built up during that time, plus principal. Both of the Stafford types of loans are obtainable through private lenders.

Perkins Loans are awarded to college students with exceptional financial need. It is a campus-based loan program using funds supplied by the federal government. This pool of money is then distributed by the financial aid office. The amounts can vary based on the amount of money that colleges have received, as well as the number of students who qualify. Currently, the maximum loan a student can receive through Perkins is $4,000 for the year. The loans are subsidized, with the federal government paying the interest during the time the student is enrolled in college, as well as the nine-month period following departure/graduation from college.

The PLUS loans are available for parents to assume the remaining cost of education for their children when other options have been exhausted. These allow for the lending entity managing the loan to make a payment to the college to satisfy part of the school bill. However, be aware that one of the conditions of these types of loans is that you have to start making monthly payments within sixty days of when the loan disbursement occurred (principal and interest). I believe good alternatives to PLUS loans are payment plans, which allow you to make your monthly payments, stay current with your child's school bill, and avoid interest charges. More about payment plans is covered later in this chapter.

Special State Programs

Each state offers unique grant programs that assist students with their educational expenses. For example, many states offer scholarships through their universities for top academic scholars. Many also offer loan repayment programs for teacher education students agreeing to serve a certain number of years in one of the public high schools after graduation (due to the shortage of teachers in many parts of the country). Another interesting program is the Southern Regional Educational Board (SREB) Common Market, which allows students to attend colleges outside of their state (but within the SREB States) if their major is not offered, and get the benefit of in-state tuition rates. Because there are so many of these special state programs, check the website for your state to find out what is offered.

APPLYING FOR GOVERNMENT AID

As mentioned earlier, the FAFSA form is the means families use to apply for government aid. If you're planning to apply for federal and state aid, be advised that you should submit the FAFSA (paper version or online) before June 30 (before your student enrolls). However, applying as soon as your previous year's 1040 is complete will allow your profile to be available to the colleges sooner. That's important because at some schools, the need-based aid is limited, so the early birds get the aid, if eligible. And this could happen before the FAFSA deadline of June 30. If your 1040s are usually delayed because of the nature of your finances, David Weliver of *SmartMoney* magazine writes, "It's completely legit to estimate tax figures based on last year's return and update them later."[2] The processing time of the FAFSA is a few weeks (quicker if you apply online). The result is a student aid report (SAR). This sheet summarizes your expected family contribution (EFC), and this information is sent to the colleges and universities that you identified were of interest at the point you completed the FAFSA. The colleges will accept this data into their systems and generate a financial aid award letter. Be aware that if you plan to apply for any institutional grants or scholarships, each college will likely need you to fill out a form just for their usage.

When you see the EFC, you may say to yourself, "They say we should be able to contribute $6,000 this year, but we don't have that amount in savings." That's not unusual. The

EFC is based upon a financial formula that looks at not only your savings, but also your earnings. The government *does* expect parents and students to contribute toward the cost. So if you're at that point right now, you need to save as much as you can before college, during college, and be prepared to be making payments after your child graduates. If you've got some time before your child starts college, you should also save as much as you can, and try to keep pace with the school bills as your student progresses toward graduation, trying to avoid loans if possible. I view loans as a last-resort option—but a decision that parents and students need to consider if necessary.

OUTSIDE SCHOLARSHIPS

More and more families are seeking out scholarships that are offered locally, regionally, and nationally through foundations, corporations, and civic organizations. Some friends of ours recently had a daughter enter a Christian liberal arts college, and through their deliberate efforts they were able to obtain $2,000 in outside scholarship money. That may not be typical of what some families receive, but it demonstrates the potential.

These outside scholarship dollars essentially represent *that much less* that your family has to contribute toward the bill. You may be asking, "How in the world do I find out about these outside scholarships?" You can find these in reference books at local libraries, by checking with local companies, civic organizations, your local church, as well as through websites such as: www.fastweb.com, www.scholarships.com, and www.findtuition.com. If your student pursues these, he should be prepared to fill out many applications, write essays, answer questions, and even interview—but for many families, the extra effort may be worth it. Once you receive word that your student is receiving outside scholarships, you'll want to notify the financial aid office of the college where he is enrolling, so they can factor that money into the overall package.

PAYMENT PLANS

Along with receiving your financial aid award letter from colleges, your family will be sent payment plan information. Some colleges offer their own payment plans, but the majority of institutions are using outside companies to manage these programs. Two of the largest of these companies are Academic Management Services (www. secure.tuitionpay.com) and Tuition Management Systems (www.afford. com).

When you sign up for these programs, you complete a simple application and include a one-time application fee. There is no interest to pay—just the amount you want to pay to the university each month. Most of the plans last for ten to eleven months. They will want you to begin payments in June or July before the college year starts. The companies give you payment coupons (like the ones you may be using to pay your mortgage note or car loan) to use in sending in your monthly payments. They also can arrange for automatic withdrawal from your checking or savings accounts. Once that period is completed toward the end of the school year, you get a break from the plan for a month or two before the next year's cycle begins again. Like much of the financial aid process, you have to sign up each year to participate.

I'm sold on these payment plans because they offer an additional option for covering the bill after financial aid. They are good for parents who have all the money up front—allowing them to disburse a month at a time, rather than all at once at the beginning of each new semester or quarter. This is good cash management because it allows possibilities for using those funds in other strategic ways. Payment plans are also good for families that don't have enough saved to pay for college because it allows them to pay as they go using current cash flow from paychecks to lessen the amount they have to take out in loans. For those in this latter category, this can be a difference maker, especially if you're short on savings and hesitant to accumulate a lot of loans. Here are a couple of financial aid scenarios including how a payment plan can fit into the mix:

Scenario One

Cost of Education	$ 24,000
Savings (parents and student)	$ – 6,000
Financial Aid (grants from all sources)	$ – 6,000
Stafford Loan	$ – 2,625
Subtotal	$ 9,375
Payment plan	$ 9,375
(10 months at $937.50 per payment)	
Balance	$ 0

Scenario Two

Cost of Education	$ 10,000
Savings (parents and student)	$ –2,000
Financial Aid (grants from all sources)	$ –5,000
(decided against loans)	$ –0
Subtotal	$ 3,000
Payment plan	$ 3,000
(10 months at $300 per payment)	
Balance	$ 0

SAVINGS PLANS

Besides regular interest-bearing savings accounts at local banking institutions, there are other means of saving for college —with some tax benefits. The first of these are Coverdell accounts. Formerly known as Education IRAs, Coverdell Educational Savings plans allow for parents to set up custodial accounts for their children for educational costs (higher education included). Currently, parents can contribute up to $2,000 per year, per child. These funds grow over time, and for people in most tax brackets, are usually tax free when cashed in for legitimate educational expenses.

Other quality savings plans for parents (and grandparents) are 529 plans. Most states offer a 529 plan, so check into those first because there may be some tax benefit if you're a resident. A website that lists the program for each state is www.collegesavings. org. Also keep in mind that your contributions grow tax deferred, and distributions for college costs come out tax free (for tax years 2002–2010). Congress will be voting on whether to extend the benefit beyond the year 2010. If they allow it to run out, the plans are still valid, except for the tax-free designation upon cash out.

Series EE U.S. savings bonds through the Treasury Department continue to be a means of putting money away for college tax free, if used for educational purposes. These bonds can be purchased online or in local banks. Just go to www. savingsbonds.gov.

My wife, Carolyn, and I have been saving for college for our children since they were born. We started out buying Series EE savings bonds, then moved to education IRAs (now known as Coverdell accounts), and in the past few years added

529 plans for each of our four children. While we've been planning in this way, it may not be enough to cover the cost—especially if they go to private colleges or universities. Therefore, we'll likely be contributing significant dollars in college payments while they are in school (especially since it looks like for one of those years, we'll have three of our four children in college), we'll use a payment plan and perhaps also need to take out some loans. We'd prefer not to use student or parent loans, but if it means the difference of them going to their top-choice college—or choosing one that is not as good a fit, we'll go ahead and take out the loans. We want to invest in our children, and we value the importance of higher education in further developing who they are becoming and how God will use them for His service and kingdom. Assuring that they each end up at the best possible college for them is of the utmost importance. So for us, helping the kids pay back loans would not be a major showstopper for us.

And speaking frankly, I'm growing a bit weary of hearing Christian parents say they don't or won't help their kids with college. It's one thing if the family is truly struggling with a devastating financial picture with loss of job(s), tragic illness, or death—but that's usually the exception. In these difficult circumstances, it is totally understandable that parents will be unable to help much. However, many parents had the means to contribute but made financial choices that did not include their children's college education. They're the parents who took a chance on an investment scheme that ended up going bad, or who built their dream house at a bad time (a few years before the kids are ready for college), or the ones who "invested" in a midlife crisis red convertible, or maybe even the ones who felt like they needed luxurious vacations. I don't know about you, but I see that as a statement of priority—what is truly valued.

I've also known parents with great fiscal discipline who have the ability to send their kids to school but their financial constraint carries over into how they view their kids' futures. They tell them they won't help with college, that they're on their own. These parents are "too tight" to let loose of the money because they're saving it for a rainy day, or want their kids to have to pay for it themselves. Matthew records the words of Jesus in the following passage:

> *Do not store up for yourselves treasures on earth, where moth and rust destroy, and where thieves break in and steal. But store up for yourselves treasures in heaven, where moth and rust do not destroy, and where thieves do not break in and steal. For where your treasure is, there your heart will be also.* (6:19–21)

If we apply this biblical narrative to the *stingy* parent, we can conclude that financial resources are to be used for kingdom work—for eternal purposes. We can also see that if we aren't inclined to share these resources with treasures we've been entrusted with (including our children), our hearts are not focused with eternity in mind—but rather on ourselves.

My fellow parents, I believe strongly that part of the resources God allows us to acquire are for us to pass along to our children. Why not give them some of it when it really matters in their lives—during college, helping them with wedding costs, assisting them in buying their first home, helping your grandkids? When you're dead—the inheritance will have minimal meaning to them or to you. Do something with your money that matters now so you all can be impacted by it.

My hope is that you will realize and embrace the importance of the undergraduate college experience and what it can mean in the life of your child(ren). And also that you will be compelled to make some changes, if necessary, in your priorities while you still have time.

Financing the college education and doing so with the intent to place your children in the best place to grow and mature in Christ is a spiritual act on your part. With that desire in your heart, know that Matthew 6:33 is an assurance to you.

But seek first his kingdom and his righteousness, and all these things will be given to you as well.

The Transition to College

Congratulations! The college that fits is in clear focus. Your student has been accepted and the countdown begins. When you find yourself at this point, a lot of effort has already gone into this process. But there is still much to do before officially enrolling. Fortunately, there are some things that you can do to help your student in the transition from high school to college.

ORIENTATION

You and your collegebound student will likely be invited to an orientation program as college approaches. Commonly, there are a couple of programs offered by colleges to assist your family in the transition to college. The first of these is an early orientation, which usually takes place in June or July on the campus. These programs allow your student to preregister for

classes, meet an academic advisor or department faculty chair-
person, make sure the school bill or payment plan is arranged,
check out the residence hall room, and perhaps even get to
meet or choose a roommate or two. By taking care of these
kinds of details during early orientation, there is less stress
when you are preparing to drop off your student "for good."
And if one or both of the parents have not visited the campus
before, this orientation gives them a chance to get familiar with
everything.

The other type of orientation is the one scheduled the first
few days on campus at the start of the freshman school year. It
gives new students and their parents a chance to get acquaint-
ed with each other and with the institution. There are usually
many things to take care of those first few days, in addition to
attending sessions that will help your student make a smooth
transition. If you've been fortunate enough to have attended
an early orientation, your student will be in much better shape
as far as taking care of all the details. If you haven't done so already, you might want to check out the churches in the area
and attend a service while you and your student are on campus
for orientation.

I can vividly remember going with my parents to drop off
my sister at Moody Bible Institute in Chicago. I was thirteen
at the time, sitting in the back seat of a 1970 Pontiac Catalina,
having been along for the two hundred-mile drive from northwest Ohio to urban Chicago. I loved it, and the city was
great—but I wasn't so sure how to handle the loss of my sister.
Although I smacked her in the arm (rather than hugging her)
as we said good-bye, I came to find out later in life that this act
of aggression was actually a sign of endearment. Fortunately,
she forgave me!

Leaving your kids at college can be difficult. I've seen the most rock-solid dads lose it as they say good-bye. It symbolizes the end of an era for us as parents. However, for our children, it's the start of an exciting future.

Parents sometimes anticipate the homesickness that occasionally happens with new college students. It's actually not that frequent of an occurrence. You'll find that your student will quickly get caught up in all the activities of college life, as well as adapting to new levels of academic expectations. It's probably more common for parents to be the ones experiencing strong emotions of separation from their children.

If you do find that your student calls or e-mails a few days or a week after school starts saying she doesn't like it and wants to come home, don't give in and let her. Yes, you got it—it's not even an option. Of course, you'll want to listen to your student to find out the reasons for her feelings, but the worst thing you can do is cave in and say, "Sure, honey, come right home to Mommy." Your student needs your reassurance that you believe in her and know that she can succeed. More time is usually needed to make the adjustment, meet new friends, and get involved. By listening, you can also give counsel about some possible ways to resolve the discomfort or suggest someone at the college who might be of assistance.

When you attend these orientation events for families, behind the scenes there is a "handing off the torch" transition that is taking place between college staff and departments. Up until now your interaction has primarily been with the admissions and financial aid offices. In this transition period, you'll begin to have more communication with student and academic services offices such as the registrar's office, student development, and the residence life office. They will send you information via e-mail and the postal service to which you'll want to give your full attention. The colleges not only provide information that's good for your student to read, but also send forms that need to be filled out to meet the requirements for enrollment. *Don't* let a bunch of these papers stack up over the summer. If your student is gone for part of the summer on a missions trip or at camp, either send the information to her or open the information and help her do what is necessary. Read each piece of mail carefully and take care of the requests for information. This helps out the offices at the college prepare for your student's arrival—but more important, it makes your student's transition a lot easier.

Just this past year at Moody, we had a high percentage of the entering students forget or neglect to get their medical forms filled out and returned to us. It was really difficult for parents to have to try to collect this type of information while standing in line at one of the departments—a thousand miles from home. That's why the forms are sent to you *before* you get to campus.

ADVISING

Colleges and universities offer academic advising through departments that specialize in helping students with their college course plan or through faculty members in the academic area your student has selected as her major. They will help counsel your student regarding the classes she needs to take and in the order they should be taken. If the college has faculty involved in advising, the relationships that can form between students and professors has the potential to be very valuable and memorable. It's one thing to sit in class with faculty members—it's another thing to get to spend some time interacting and sharing one on one.

My academic advisor in college, Dr. Robert Clark, was a veteran in the field of my undergraduate major, Christian education. He had written books, spoken at professional conferences, and taught for years. I got to spend time with him in class, as well as after class. He helped me maneuver through the curriculum, as well as giving me a few well-deserved reality checks. I had a chance to see Dr. Clark in Littleton, Colorado, a couple of years ago, and it was wonderful to connect again after nearly twenty years. At his insistence, I got to call him by his first name, "Bob," but more important, I got to thank him for his investment in me. He was quite complimentary to me given where I was as an undergraduate student. He remembered me lacking motivation, drive, and being easily sidetracked from my studies to extracurricular activities. As opposed to my wife, Carolyn, who was named to "Who's Who" during college and had all kinds of direction and focus, I probably could have been classified as "Who's That?" But God used the stretching experiences in college and a select group of people like my advisor who believed in and encouraged me. The relationship with him made a difference in my life. As a parent, think through your college experience, whether you went to a huge university or a small college; did faculty help shape your experience? Advising relationships are as meaningful to college students today as they were twenty years ago.

RESIDENCE LIFE CHOICE

The choice of where to live during the college years is fairly significant and can play a major part in how well your child does in college. Of course, if your daughter is taking classes to complete a degree via the Internet or studying at a local college —*your home* may continue to be her residence. Depending on your student's needs, this can work out well, or it may not be the best situation.

A fairly large number of students choose to live in residence halls, a.k.a. dorms. These college-owned buildings provide not only rooms, but also supervision for your collegebound student. Residence halls have traditionally included bedrooms, bathrooms, central lounges, and storage. At large universities, there is usually a central dining room for food service right there in the dorm. There are usually between two or three students in each room with each having their own bed and desk. Some colleges have suites with four students sharing two rooms and an adjoining bathroom. In recent years, colleges have been moving toward apartment-style accommodations to better meet the needs of today's students. These apartments are more private with additional living space to accommodate the things students like to bring with them to college, such as computers, microwaves, and surround-sound media systems. Even with the different layout, apartments owned by the college or university may still provide the supervision that traditional dorms offer.

Fraternities and sororities constitute the living arrangements for what is known as Greek life on some colleges and universities. Greek organizations are a nationwide network of campus-based organizations that serve larger purposes than just housing of college students. In many Christian circles, we automatically assume that sororities and fraternities are dens of iniquity, based upon the movies and television shows we've seen. While certainly that reputation is well deserved around many campuses, we shouldn't assume that *all* Greek houses are beer gardens and serve no purpose other than providing an environment in which to get drunk. Some of our Christian kids are living in these environments and serving an important role of salt and light, as described by Matthew 5:13–14. While it may not be the first choice for your daughter or son, realize that this is a residence option that needs the light of the gospel. How else, other than through some of our brightest and best Christian youth, will this take place?

Off-campus housing is used by a growing number of college students. Typically these "just off campus" facilities are apartment buildings or houses that students rent from landlords. It's common for undergrads to stay in the campus residence halls the first couple of years, and then as upperclassmen move off campus to one of these other options. However, before you assume that your student can move off campus, have her check with the residence life office at the college to see what kinds of residence requirements are in place. In some institutions, they expect students to be in residence all four years.

Just keep in mind that apart from living at home, your student will be out from under your direct oversight at these different residence hall situations. That may be a bit unsettling, but if you've done a good job preparing them for life, you may be surprised how well they do at things like laundry, money management, entertainment choices, and connecting with a local church.

EXTRACURRICULAR CHOICES

The activities that your student chooses to get involved with have a major effect on the transition and adjustment to college. Former U.S. Commissioner of Education Ernest Boyer observed, "The effectiveness of the undergraduate experience relates to the quality of campus life. It is directly linked to the time students spend on campus and to the quality of their involvement in activities."[1] College is more than just going to class and meeting curricular requirements. Don't get me wrong—academics are important and are the primary purpose for college, but outside involvements will help assure that your student grows and develops in many different ways. Extracurricular activities allow for some important interaction to take place outside the classroom. Even if your student does not live on campus, there are usually ways for her to get involved in activities. But beware—some college students get so enamored with the freedom that college life provides that they get *too involved* in extracurricular activities, which can hinder academic performance. The key is finding a balance to all the college life responsibilities.

SERVICE AND MINISTRY OPPORTUNITIES

Tied to extracurricular activities are opportunities for Christian students to get involved for faith-based purposes. You'll be thrilled to know that there are many ways for them to get involved in ministry. In fact, the issue is not "Is there enough to do?" it is "How does one choose between so many ministry possibilities?" It depends on the student and the accessible opportunities. On a Christian college campus, there is a department that specializes in helping students get linked into ministry. In these contexts, that ministry may be weekly or monthly—or take the form of a short-term missions trip. While visiting International Christian College in Glasgow,

Scotland, last year, I met a student who developed a ministry to skateboarders in the public parks. What an innovative way to integrate into a culture and touch the lives of young people needing the Lord.

The opportunities for involvement in ministry do not stop with faith-based institutions. While enrolled in my master's program at the University of Tennessee in Knoxville, as a part of one of my practicums I did a study to identify and learn about all the ministry groups surrounding the campus. It was amazing to see all these groups and what they were doing to advance the cause of Christ through evangelism, discipleship, mentoring, tutoring, meeting physical needs, and more. While none of these groups was a part of the university, they were effective in meeting the needs of students and the community at large.

RELATIONSHIPS

While it may not be homesickness *per se,* many college-bound students underestimate the degree to which they will miss their family and friends. The relationships they've built their entire lives with family, neighbors, youth group, and school friends suddenly change as they head off to college. Even if your student is staying at home and commuting to college, relationships are different because most of their friends head off in different directions for college or work, and it's just not the same anymore. For most students this transition isn't overwhelming because they've moved into a new environment and gotten busy with classes, extracurricular activities, and ministry opportunities. In a sense, they've replaced the old relationships with new relationships at college. However, some will struggle and find this transition debilitating. Not all of our children are adventurous, and some find adjusting to new places and people very difficult. You may find that your collegebound student isn't necessarily looking forward to the new place—not because there's anything wrong with it, but because it's different. Sometimes the new environment just doesn't seem as good as the old one. For one, your relationship with your student will change in some ways because, naturally, you won't be on campus.

Of course, there are a few families who are exceptions to the rule. In one instance, I remember some parents that went to college *with* their son. Yes, they loaded up the truck and moved to the same city as the college their son had chosen. The father's retirement from the military coincided with their son's graduation from high school, so they were seeking a new base of operation. They had moved many times before as a family, so they thought, "Why not stay together awhile longer?" If some of us suggested moving to college with our kids, the response wouldn't necessarily be positive! However, it may be a good way to shock your student into consciousness some Saturday morning—try it. Once her eyeballs stop rolling and a couple of huffs occur, you might open up some dialogue about the impending changes she'll experience in relationships.

Fellow parents, we play an important role in preparing our children for this change. This is one of those aspects of preparedness in which we need to be actively engaged—helping our children understand the forthcoming changes as a result of going to college. We can't assume that our kids will automatically be able to anticipate and understand the changes that they will go through, but there are some practical ways you can help them.

Saying good-bye to family and friends from school and church is often overlooked in the transition. It can be difficult, but it's important to do because in life, relationships not only have starting points and certain seasons of interaction, but also regularly come to an end. You might want to consider throwing your collegebound student a party with friends and/or family to give her a chance to reflect on the past *and* celebrate future opportunities. Being able to show love and appreciation to people who have meant a lot to your child is a wonderful affirmation of what God accomplishes through others. To a large degree, when your student goes to college, things with her friends will never be quite the same when she comes back to visit. While family usually stays in contact through holiday celebrations, friends scatter to many places. The closest thing to reconnecting and reliving some of the past is at the high school reunions, but even then, not everybody returns. Sure, your student will stay connected with close friends through instant messaging, texting, and e-mail—but even then those relationships fade over time. It's not because anything is wrong, it's just that new friendships are developed. Saying good-bye helps teens adjust mentally and prepare to move on to a new stage or season of life.

By the way, it can be very tough when parents say good-bye before driving away from taking their child to college! For over twenty years, I've been helping recruit, admit, and transition college students, and it's obvious that it can be very difficult on the parents. When I was new to the higher education profession, I thought it was a bit overreactive for the parents to be crying when leaving their kids at college. I thought they should be in a celebratory mood upon dropping them off (maybe because that's how my parents felt upon leaving me at college). But as I've grown older and gotten closer to sending *my* children to college, I better understand the emotional reality and parent-child bond.

This past August, as parents were here in Chicago listening to Moody's president share about how well the institution would take care of their kids and tell them what they could do to encourage them to get a good start, a wave of emotion swept over the crowd. While many moms were the ones quietly sobbing, several of the dads broke down later in the evening as they were reunited with their kids following the dedication service. After this event, I followed some parents out of the auditorium who obviously had just said good-bye to their student before going home. Leaving campus was very hard, not because of Moody, but because they were leaving an important commodity at this school—their precious child. Probably without realizing how deflated they looked, they walked toward the parking garage, arms around each other, leaning on each other, and whispering words of comfort to each other.

It's abnormal not to feel some of this, but parents need to try to somewhat keep it together when saying good-bye to their son or daughter. It can make it harder on the student's transition to think her parents are basket cases.

It's not that you want to shut down your emotions—you definitely want your children to know how much you love them, will miss them, and how proud you are of them! They need to know that you'll stand behind them in their choice of this college and their success in earning their degree. It's time for you, once again, to be their biggest cheerleader.

BUILDING NEW RELATIONSHIPS

Without interfering too much, you'll want to help encourage new college relationships. Once you know who your student's roommate(s) will be, help the two or three of them get preconnected. Doing so gives them a chance to not only get to know each other, but also provides a chance to talk about room layout, furnishings, and who's bringing what items (mini-fridge, microwave, stereo). As mentioned earlier, many colleges offer an early orientation or summer orientation programs, which are great opportunities for your student to get connected to new friends and also to learn who the key people are at the college or university. This experience almost always gives your student a lot more confidence in her college choice and the sense that she is on top of things.

STAY IN CONTACT

After you drop off your child at college, *don't* phone or e-mail her immediately. Wait a day or so, largely because the college personnel are keeping her *very* busy all day long. Your student is staying up late getting to know new people and does need some sleep. It will be hard for you to wait, but giving your child a chance to spread her wings, get used to their new surroundings, and settle in can be very healthy in the long run. You don't want to be smothering. If your student is initiating the calls and e-mails, try and keep the emphasis on the new environment and provide encouragement for any difficult moments (if any have arisen). If she is homesick and ready to depart college, tell her no. It's not that you don't love her, it's that you don't want her to leave and pass up this

great opportunity. Troubleshoot what the source of prob-
lem(s) might be, and behind the scenes, work with college
personnel to find help for your student. The student development personnel are typically the ones who have all the
connections to solve transition issues. In very rare cases,
some students do leave college early in the semester because
of extreme circumstances—if that's best. However, most students will work through some adjustments and emerge as
stronger and more confident individuals.

You can expect your student to call and e-mail less frequently after the first couple of months. Some friends of ours
are experiencing this very phenomenon this year, as their
daughter is getting busier and more ingrained in the culture of
the college she is attending. You'll find that your student becomes so busy with class requirements, extracurricular involvement, work, and socializing, that she has little time to
connect with you. A practical way to keep in contact and com-
municate your love is to send the old-fashioned care package.
That's right—college students still enjoy receiving boxes from
home with a caring note, a few dollars for laundry or pizza,
and goodies. If it's fresh-baked cookies or pie that your student
is hungering for, be aware that these items tend to get pulver-
ized in the shipping process. You might want to send snacks
that are already packaged, and by all means using shipping
peanuts and bubble wrap in the box to alleviate some of the
breakage. If you're short on time, some colleges will offer parents a service where they do the baking of goodies and deliver
them to your student at a modest charge. It's great—the staff
does all the work and you get all the credit!

Another way to stay connected with children while they
are in college is through writing letters or e-mail. Yes, it takes

time, but it is *oh* so meaningful. A friend of mine committed to write a letter per week to his three daughters while they were away at college (they were not enrolled simultaneously). Each Monday, he jotted down some thoughts and sent the letters through the postal service. He shared with me that the letters were fairly simple, just a chronicle of what was happening at home and encouraging his daughters with things he was learning from the Word. By being deliberate about staying in touch, it spoke volumes to them about their value—that he would take the time out of his busy professional and personal life to write. They reflect back on those letters with great fondness.

I encourage you to think about some creative ways you can stay in contact and be an encouragement to your college student.

ATTEND PARENTS' WEEKEND

A growing number of colleges are offering parents' weekends in the fall semester to give families an opportunity to reunite after a month or two of college. I recommend these events to parents, especially the first couple of years of college. This is a great opportunity to see how students are doing in the adjustment to college life, get to know their friends, and find out what they are learning. Usually, it's good on all accounts, but occasionally you'll notice some negative behaviors emerging and those need to be confronted early on. For example, you need to know if your student is connecting with a campus ministry group and a local church. You need to find out if she is going to class, showing up for work, and getting some sleep. Also, is your student hanging out with other

Christians in healthy relationships? These are things to identify early on, and if there needs to be intervention, you can work
alongside of the student services staff, campus ministry leaders, or local churches to assist. Another purely practical reason
to go to these parents' weekends is to bring your student the
next season of clothing. Seasons change and moderate most
anywhere and some different clothes are needed. In the
process of attending these parents' weekends, you get to know
more about the college, as well as make some new friends with
other parents of college students. Who knows, you may be related to a couple of them someday!

LETTING GO

In closing this chapter out, let me add a reminder that the
work we have invested in our children to shepherding them in
godly ways is a changing, lifelong process. The childhood period of their lives is temporary and is supposed to prepare them
for adulthood. Our nurturing is intended to build them up to
not only be well-adjusted individuals, but also infuse in them a
spiritual dimension that permeates all of who they are, what
God created them to become, and what they do. It's common
for teens to have a compartment of their lives that is spiritual—
but it is among many dimensions of their lives. Believers
should have a biblical worldview that forms every other aspect
of their lives. While they (and we as parents) will have the
struggle against the flesh, we need to be passionate about staying "in the Spirit." If we can see that achieved in their lives, our
children will be well prepared for the college or university God
has for them. However, regardless of how they are doing, we
have to release our young adults and realize that our ways of

influence are changing. We certainly need to stay connected, but our role is more supportive.

That can be a bit scary, but fortunately you have a God who loves them and cares for them in ways that are beyond our reach as parents. Be assured that the biblical basis you have given and modeled to them will not be wasted. Proverbs 22:6 says, "Train a child in the way he should go, and when he is old he will not turn from it." With that confidence, we can entrust our young adults to Him, let go, and give them wings to soar—much like a mother eagle does with her maturing eaglets.

A Word for Collegebound Students

College life is exciting, and you have a lot to look forward to as you progress into higher education. As you consider the possibilities, I just want to emphasize a point that is very important to consider as you enter the next season of your life. Your walk with Christ needs to be a priority—even more so than during your high school years.

The college years are typically transitional ones for students —moving from their families through the gateway to adulthood. The four to five years it takes for most students to complete their college degrees are pivotal to their futures. Obviously, people go to college to gain more knowledge about the world and themselves and to focus on a career for the future. But students also work part-time, socialize, and get involved in extracurricular activities.

As you go to college, you will find it amazing how many things will be clamoring for your time and attention. Because so much of it is appealing, it's easy to get involved in a lot of college-related activities, find yourself overwhelmed, and then get behind in your studies and your walk with Christ. You need to guard yourself from losing perspective on what is most important. An unbalanced, undisciplined life is folly in the sight of God. But it is possible to live a balanced life and still enjoy each day. Colossians 1:10–12 provides a glimpse of what this looks like:

> *And we pray this in order that you may live a life worthy of the Lord and may please him in every way: bearing fruit in every good work, growing in the knowledge of God, being strengthened with all power according to his glorious might so that you might have great endurance and patience, and joyfully giving thanks to the Father, who has qualified you to share in the inheritance of the saints in the kingdom of light.*

One of the most challenging things to do in college is to develop an even deeper relationship with Christ. At state schools or non-Christian institutions, there is what feels like a gravitational pull away from God because of the lack of affirmation He receives in classes and dorm life. It can be a struggle for Christian students to keep Him first in day-to-day university life. In fact, some grow so disillusioned with their faith in light of the influences against it that they subtly throw in the towel and "chuck it." And at Christian colleges, it can be hard to grow in a personal relationship with Christ because the tendency is to rely on the Christian atmosphere (curriculum, faculty, friends, chapels, and outreach) for strength. *So we can assume that it's hard to grow in Christ, regardless of where a person goes to college, right?* Wherever we are in life, there are always distractions to our relationship with Christ. The Evil One doesn't want you to have a vibrant, growing relationship with Christ Jesus; rather he would prefer that you get busy with everything else in university life.

The point is that walking with Christ needs to be an *intentional* priority. We want to be close to Him because of His great love for us, which He has demonstrated in so many ways. We want to get to know the One who created us, saved us from our sins by His death and resurrection, and redeemed us to new and eternal life. Isn't it true that He is and has always been there for us, but we're the ones who tend to get distracted and lose interest? As we all know, any relationship takes time, which means it's important that you as a college student learn to carve out the best part of your day to study God's Word, meditate, journal, and pray. A quiet place and time are usually best to focus on Him, which on most college campuses is often easier to find in the morning. It's almost eerie how quiet things are before noon. An uncrowded lounge, park bench, or coffee shop can be a good place to read God's Word, meditate, and prepare for the day. Certainly, you will want to keep the Bible as the cornerstone of your devotional life, but look to find other tools that can help you in your study. Many college students use one of the plans available to read through the Bible in a year. Also, there are devotional books, Bible study guides, and current-issue oriented studies to supplement spiritual growth. And we've just been talking about personal study. Other indispensable means to growing in Christ include group Bible studies, as well as accountability and mentoring relationships.

Group Bible studies can provide nonthreatening opportunities not only for Christian students to get together to grow, but they are also venues to invite nonbelievers to learn more about Jesus Christ. Perhaps you will be the impetus to start and lead Bible studies to stay in the Word and encourage others to grow in their relationship with God. Even on Christian college campuses, students form groups to study the Bible. On secular campuses, Bible studies are a spiritual lifeline to keep your faith intact. There are so many opposing forces that represent antagonistic views of Christianity and its followers that fellow believers are needed for support. Mentorships are essentially one-on-one relationships where you get together with another Christian for support and encouragement. Along with Bible study and prayer, these relationships can provide opportunities for open sharing about how each of you is doing. There are also small groups that do similar kinds of things, which are often referred to as accountability groups. Many do book studies on topics such as integrity, purity, attributes of God, or the fruit of the Spirit, just to name a few. More often than not, these mentorships and accountability groups are same-gender to allow for more open discussion of issues unique to women and men. These close relationships are worth the time invested and important to your growing faith.

Proclaiming Christ doesn't have to be a programmed activity that's expected or planned. Sharing Him with others should be a natural part of who we are as believers and easily woven into our conversations. The college atmosphere is a great place to share your faith because there are so many students searching for who they are and answering some important questions about life. It's at this point in their lives that people establish if faith will play any part in their lives in the future. For those who come to college as non-Christians, they may have blinders on about faith in Christ. If no one tells them about Him, how will they accept Him as Savior? In fact, those without Christ can see faith as foolish. Paul confirms this in 1 Corinthians 1:18: "For the message of the cross is foolishness to those who are perishing, but to those of us who are being saved it is the power of God." In the verse that comes next (v. 19), what God says that He will ultimately do is especially pertinent to higher education: "I will destroy the wisdom of the wise; the intelligence of the intelligent I will frustrate." The Holy Spirit is alive on college campuses and is drawing people to God. He is drawing back the curtain of blindness and revealing His truth. Human understanding cannot transcend the mind of God or His eternal plan. It takes His intervention and students who are willing to step out and share their faith. A couple of verses that capture this passion for sharing this good news are found in Colossians 1:28–29:

> *We proclaim him, admonishing and teaching everyone with all wisdom, so that we may present everyone perfect in Christ. To this end I labor, struggling with all his energy, which so powerfully works in me.*

Serving God is our privilege. In fact, it should be a generous impulse. Many opportunities will come your way during college to serve others in the name of Christ. Ministering in homeless shelters, tutoring underprivileged youth, digging wells in Africa so people can have a more reliable water source, building homes for Habitat for Humanity, teaching the Scriptures in backyard Bible clubs, working with teens in church youth groups, helping boys or girls memorize Scripture at Awana clubs—these are just a few of the kinds of service ministries where you can play a part. Christian colleges have departments that help coordinate individual and group ministries local to the institution, as well as cross-cultural ministry opportunities. At public and non-Christian institutions the area campus ministry groups offer a variety of involvements to get students linked into service opportunities for Christ. There is something about serving others in the name of Christ that emblazons our faith and makes us even more excited about our relationship with Him. Regardless of the type of institution you attend, stay engaged in the lives of others.

Take advantage of your years in college to walk with Him, proclaim Him, and serve Him. Setting these as priorities will matter for eternity.

Internet Resources

Described throughout the book are valuable resources available on the Internet. This list of college-related Web resources is not exhaustive, but it does include many of the major sites. Not only can you access a vast array of information on the Internet, but also you can do so in your own time frame and in a convenient setting. The resources listed are organized in such a way as to allow you to find what you need depending on your stage in the college search process.

College Guides Search/Comparison Tools

Peterson's Guides:	www.petersons.com
Princeton Review:	www.princetonreview.com
Christian College Mentor:	www.christiancollegementor.org
CollegeNet:	www.collegenet.com

College Board: www.collegeboard.com
    (see College Quickfinder and College Matchmaker)
Collegeview: www.collegeview.com
Xap: www.xap.com
Schools in the USA: www.schoolsintheusa.com

Online Campus Tours

www.campustours.com

Institution Types

State Universities: www.aascu.org
Community Colleges: www.aacc.nche.edu
Tribal Colleges: www.aihec.org
Coast Guard Academy: www.cga.org
Naval Academy: www.nadn.navy.mil
Merchant Marine Academy: www.usmma.edu
West Point: www.usma.edu
Air Force Academy: www.usafa.af.mil
National Association of
    Independent Colleges and Universities: www.naicu.edu
Council for Christian Colleges & Universities
    (Christian liberal arts institutions):   www.cccu.org
Association for Biblical Higher Education
    (Bible colleges):   www.abhe.org

Military Opportunities

U.S. Military: www.myfuture.com

Accrediting Associations

Council for Higher Education Accreditation: www.chea.org

College Tests

ACT: www.actstudent.org

SAT: www.collegeboard.com

College Credit Options

AP or CLEP: www.collegeboard.com

Interest Inventory

Crown Financial Ministries *Career Direct:* www.crown.org

Focus on the Family *The Call:* www.focusonyourchild.org

Common Applications

www.commonapp.org

www.xap.com

Study Abroad Programs

Educational Directories Unlimited: www.studyabroad.com

Council for Christian Colleges

& Universities: www.bestsemester.com

Saving for College

The Smart Student Guide: www.finaid.org/savings

U.S. Savings Bonds: www.savingsbonds.gov

Financial Aid

Smart Student Guide: www.finaid.org
FAFSA: www.fafsa.ed.gov
Profile: https://profileonline.collegeboard.com

Financial Aid Estimators

www.finaid.org
www.princetonreview.com/college/finance/efc

Payment Plans

AMS: www.secure.tuitionpay.com
TMS: www.afford.com

State 529 Savings Plans

www.collegesavings.org

Scholarships

National Merit Scholarship Program: www.nationalmerit.org
Fastweb: www.fastweb.com
Princeton Review: www.findtuition.com
Scholarship Experts: www.scholarshipexperts.com
FindTuition: www.findtuition.com
Scholarships: www.scholarships.com

Program for Preparing Christian Students for Secular Institutions

Summit Ministries: www.summit.org

Options for Students Not Ready for College

Torchbearer Schools	www.capernwray.org.uk
Word of Life Bible Institute	www.wol.org/biblei
Fort Wilderness *In Pursuit*	www.fortwilderness.com

Trends in Occupations/Career Descriptions

Occupational Outlook Handbook:	www.bls.gov/oco/

Notes

Chapter 1: Knowing Your Role and Your Student

1. Western Interstate Commission for Higher Education (WICHE), *Knocking at the College Door: Projections of High School Graduates by State, Income, and Race/Ethnicity, 1988–2018* (Boulder, Col.: WICHE, 2003). http://www.wiche.edu/resources

2. Tedd Tripp, *Shepherding a Child's Heart: Parents Handbook* (Wapwallopen, Penn.: Shepherd Press, 2001), 134. Used by permission.

3. Alexander W. Astin, *Four Critical Years* (San Francisco: Jossey-Bass, 1977).

4. Gary L. Railsback, "An Exploratory Study of Religiosity and Related Outcomes Among College Students" (dissertation, UCLA, 1994).

5. Steve Henderson, "The Impact of Student Religion and College Affiliation on Student Religiosity" (dissertation, University of Arkansas, 2003), 150.

6. Steve Henderson (presentation at the Critical Concerns Conference for Chief Enrollment Officers, Tampa, Fla., January 5, 2005).

7. Railsback, 59.

8. J. Budziszewski, *How to Stay Christian in College: An Interactive Guide to Keeping the Faith* (Colorado Springs: NavPress, 1999), 23. Used by permission. www.navpress.com. All rights reserved.

9. American College Testing Program, "National Dropout Rates, 2003," ACT Institutional Data File, accessable in David Arendale, "Review of Successful

Practices in Teaching and Learning," (critical review, University of Minnesota-Twin Cities, 2004), www.tc.umn.edu/~arend011/teachlearn.pdf

Chapter 2: An Overview of the Process

1. Don Hossler, and K. Gallagher, "Studying Student College Choice: A Three-Phase Model and the Implication for Policy Makers," *College and University*, 2, no. 3 (1987): 207–21.

2. Don Hossler, Jack Schmit, and Nick Vesper, *Going to College: How Social, Economic, and Educational Factors Influence the Decisions Students Make* (Baltimore, Md.: Johns Hopkins University Press, 1999), 28. Used by permission.

3. Don Hossler, J. Braxton, and G. Coopersmith, "Understanding Student College Choice," *Higher Education: Handbook of Theory and Research* (Agathon Press) 5 (1989): 231–88.

4. J. B. Blackburn, "The Search Stage of Student College Choice: How Students Discover the Range of College Consideration Sets" (dissertation, Baylor University, December 2000).

5. National Association for College Admission Counseling (NACAC) "2003–2004 State of College Admissions Report," (Alexandria, Va.: NACAC, 2004), 38. Used by permission.

Chapter 3: The World of Possibilities

1. Thomas D. Snyder, Alexandra G. Tan, and Charlene M. Hoffman, *Digest of Education Statistics, 2003,* ch. 3 Postsecondary Education, (2004): table 247, http://nces.ed.gov/programs/digest/d03/tables/dt247.asp (accessed January 22, 2005).

2. Ibid., table 220, http://nces.ed.gov/programs/digest/d03/tables/dt220.asp

Chapter 4: Institutional Types

1. "The Chronicle Survey of Public Opinion on Higher Education" *Chronicle of Higher Education,* vol. L, no. 352004 (May 7, 2004): A12–A13, http://chronicle.com/stats/higheredpoll/2004/attitudes.htm

2. John Dawson, "Irreligious Studies," *World,* 25 September 2004: 34–35. Used by permission.

3. Thomas D. Snyder, Alexandra G. Tan, and Charlene M. Hoffman, *Digest of Education Statistics, 2003,* ch. 3 Postsecondary Education, (2004): table 247, http://nces.ed.gov/programs/digest/d03/tables/dt247.asp

4. I. Elaine Allen, and Jeff Seaman, *Sizing the Opportunity: The Quality and Extent of On-Line Education in the United States, 2002 and 2003* (Needham, Mass.: The Sloan Consortium, 2003), 1. Used by permission. http://www.sloan-c.org/resources/sizing_opportunity.pdf

5. Ibid., 3.

Chapter 5: Criteria for Narrowing the Options

1. E. G Bogue, and R. L. Saunders, *The Evidence for Quality* (San Francisco: Jossey-Bass, 1992), 20. Used by permission.

Chapter 6: The Campus Visit

1. Art & Science Group, LLC, "Campus Visit Drives College Choice," *StudentPoll* (Baltimore) 5, no. 5, January 2004. Used by permission. http://www.artsci.com/StudentPOLL/v5n5/publishers_note.htm

2. Jay Mathews, "Parents Casting a Shadow Over College Applicants," *Washington Post,* 10 July 2004, http://www.washingtonpost.com (accessed January 21, 2005).

Chapter 7: The Admissions Process

1. Maureen Feighan, "College Web Applications Rise," *Detroit News,* 19 September 2004, http://www.detnews.com/2004/metro/0409/19/e01-277659.htm (accessed December 12, 2004).

2. Bonnie Miller Rubin, "Parents Turn Up Heat When Colleges Turn Down Kids," *Chicago Tribune,* 9 April 2004.

3. Elizabeth F. Farrell, "In the Admissions Game, Students Change the Rules," *Chronicle of Higher Education,* 50, no. 43 (July 2004), A31–A32.

Chapter 8: The Cost of College

1. Thomas D. Snyder, Alexandra G. Tan, and Charlene M. Hoffman, *Digest of Education Statistics, 2003,* ch. 3 Postsecondary Education, (2004): table 315, http://nces.ed.gov/programs/digest/d03/tables/dt315.asp

2. Sandy Baum, and Kathleen Payea, "Education Pays 2004," (New York, NY: The College Board, 2004): 7. Used by permission. http://www.collegeboard.com/prod_ downloads/press/cost04/EducationPays2004.pdf

Chapter 9: Financing the Educational Investment

1. Investment Company Institute (ICI), "Profile of Households Saving for College," Fall 2003 (Washington, DC), http://www.ici.org/stats/res/rpt_03_college_saving.pdf

2. David Weliver, "Ten Things College Financial Aid Offices Won't Tell You," *SmartMoney* 13, no. 11 (February 2004): 63–67, Used by permission. http://www.smartmoney.com/10things/index.cfm?story=feb2004

Chapter 10: The Transition to College

1. Ernest Boyer, *College: The Undergraduate Experience in America: The Carnegie Foundation for the Advancement of Teaching* (San Francisco: HarperCollins, 1987), 191. Used by permission.

SINCE 1894, Moody Publishers has been dedicated to equip and motivate people to advance the cause of Christ by publishing evangelical Christian literature and other media for all ages, around the world. Because we are a ministry of the Moody Bible Institute of Chicago, a portion of the proceeds from the sale of this book go to train the next generation of Christian leaders.

If we may serve you in any way in your spiritual journey toward understanding Christ and the Christian life, please contact us at www.moodypublishers.com.

"All Scripture is God-breathed and is useful for teaching, rebuking, correcting and training in righteousness, so that the man of God may be thoroughly equipped for every good work."

—*2 TIMOTHY 3:16, 17*

MOODY
PUBLISHERS

THE NAME YOU CAN TRUST®

COLLEGEBOUND TEAM

ACQUIRING EDITOR
Mark Tobey

COPY EDITOR
Ali Childers

BACK COVER COPY
Lisa Ann Cockrel

COVER DESIGN
John Hamilton,
The DesignWorks Group, Inc.
www.thedesignworksgroup.com

INTERIOR DESIGN
BlueFrog Design

PRINTING AND BINDING
Versa Press, Inc.

The typeface for the text of this book is
AGaramond